THE TRUE SPIRITUAL BLESSING

Dapo Benzoe

Unless otherwise indicated, all scripture references are taken from the
New King James Version (NKJV) of the Holy Bible.

Publisher's note: This maiden edition from LivingScribe has been structured in a simple format to cater for readers of every possible level. Words, expressions and sentence structure may bear a strong persuasive accent, but by no means compromise the reader's own distinct reason.

THE TRUE SPIRITUAL BLESSING

ISBN: 978-0-9571306-0-9
Printed in the United Kingdom
©2011 by Dapo Benzoe

Published by LivingScribe

Contact:
Dapo Benzoe
T: +44 (0)7737587170
E: dapo@livingscribe.org

All rights reserved. No part of this book may be reproduced
or transmitted in any form or by any means - electronic, mechanical, including
photocopying, recording, or by any information storage and
retrieval system, without permission in writing from the publisher.

CONTENTS

Foreword

Introduction

1	Entering The Kingdom Of God	11
2	Adam's Original Purpose	21
3	Blessed Are The Poor In Spirit	25
4	Blessed Are Those Who Mourn	29
5	Blessed Are The Meek	33
6	Blessed Are Those Who Hunger And Thirst For Righteousness	39
7	Blessed Are The Merciful	49
8	Blessed Are The Pure In Heart	57
9	Blessed Are The Peacemakers	63
10	Blessed Are Those Who Are Persecuted For Righteousness Sake	69
11	The Crown Receivers	81
	Conclusion	87
	Appendix	89

Now thanks be unto God, who always causes us to triumph in Christ, and makes manifest the **fragrance of His knowledge** by us in every place.

2 Corinthians 2vs14

Foreword

I have been privileged to know Pastor Dapo Benzoe for almost two decades, first as a committed believer and worker in our Ministry then in the last thirteen years as a Senior Minister in World Harvest Chrisitan Centre, UK.

Pastor Dapo Benzoe has been graced by God like Paul of Tarsus with a unique revelation and insight into the New Creation Realities. In this simple but profound book, the author highlights what the ultimate destiny of every believer is - to be conformed to the Image of Christ and what we must do to attain this goal!

This book is not for the carnal, worldly, materialistic and mesmerized believer, but for only those who love Jesus and are pursuing the Kingdom at all Cost.

I highly recommend this book both to all believers and those in Christian leadership!

Pastor Wale Babatunde
General Overseer
World Harvest Christian Centre

INTRODUCTION

"**Blessed be the God and Father of our Lord Jesus Christ who has blessed us with every spiritual blessing in the heavenly places in Christ; just as He chose us in Him before the foundation of the world that we should be Holy and without blame before Him in love having predestined us to adoption as sons by Jesus Christ to Himself according to the good pleasure of His will to the praise of the glory of His grace by which He made us accepted in the beloved.**"[1]

If one were to have a child and a hope that he or she would become a medical doctor at some time in the future, then one has desired something good for one's offspring, concerned that the child would grow up to have a secure profession and better opportunities for progression in life. Although parents may have these or similar visions for their children, the children themselves are unlikely to appreciate this because of their young age and their inability to see the bigger picture. In all probability, in practise, all that most children appreciate at this early stage of life is their immediate surroundings, playing with toys, going to playgrounds and eating food. But in twenty years time, these same children would, hopefully, have outgrown these childish desires, may well have become career-minded, could have developed their own ambition to be a medical Doctor, or some other profession of good standing, and will surely have become self motivated.

However, before these young people grow to maturity and begin to appreciate their loving parents' plans and visions for them, it

---

1 Ephesians 1. 3-6

will have proved necessary to guide them through various stages of the formal education system - nursery school, primary school, secondary school, and college/university. In addition, the child will have had to learn life, social skills and discipline both at home and in school. During all of these stages of a child's development, they will at times feel burdened, unwilling to continue and even wonder in their minds why they should have to go through all of this. However, good parents will not give up on the child because they can see what the child cannot see due to youth and immaturity. Whilst a child sees disciplined routine as a pain and something to rail against, parents see it as opportunity to encourage, motivate and to seek to explain the blessings attached to each stage of education. They offer explanation and illustration as to how eventually the child will reap the reward of a good profession earned through discipline and a willingness to learn.

Just to re-emphasis, children only see their immediate need which usually are playing, eating etc, but the parent sees beyond into the childrens future and so to the parent, the children are blessed and opportuned as they go through the necessary phases of learning such as:

Nursery School
Primary School
Secondary School
College
University
Yielding to correction and all discipline requirements

We believers are just like children, all we can see today and appreciate are the things of this world - the materialism, glamour and comfort that this world gives.

When the Lord Jesus Christ was proclaiming certain Blessings in the Sermon on the Mount[2], He had the vision of eternity in mind. He knew that in the beginning the whole universe had been programmed to yield in service and obedience to the children of God who were created in the image and likeness of God.

---

2 Matthew 5:1-11

The earth had only been programmed to respond to people in the image and likeness of God and not people of 'flesh and dust' who occupy the earth today.

Just as the child would need to go through various phases of development to qualify as a medical doctor, we as believers are required to undergo the following tests of character to be conformed to the image of God which is Christ Himself. This will qualify us to fully exercise dominion on earth with Christ Jesus in His coming Kingdom. We need to experience what it means to:

Be Poor In Spirit

Mourn

Be Merciful

Hunger And Thirst For Righteousness

Be Pure In Heart

Be Peacemakers

Be Persecuted For Righteousness Sake

Be Falsely Accused And Evil Spoken Of.

Man in the image and likeness of God, is the only one who has a 'legal' right to exercise control over this earth and the universe and that Man is Christ. The only ones who would qualify to join Him are those members of His body who will prevail in this world and allow the Spirit of God to mould them into the image of Christ.

Since His word is eternal and true, the whole earth and universe is waiting for the emergence of people in God's image and likeness. Indeed, that is our destiny as Christians, to reflect the image of God through Christ, by the work of the Holy Spirit in us, as we yield to Him.

In this book, the believer will gain tremendous insight into the mind of God concerning His word in the Sermon on the Mount. The blessings mentioned are not what most would consider as blessings and that is because this present natural world has a system that is contrary to the principles of God. In fact, the Lord says "For as the heavens are higher than the earth, so are My ways higher than your ways, and My thoughts than your thoughts."[3]

---

3 Isaiah 55:9

Chapter One

Entering the Kingdom of God

"Most assuredly I say to you, unless one is born again, he cannot see the kingdom of God. Most assuredly, I say to you, unless one is born of water and the Spirit, he cannot enter the kingdom of God."[4]

When Adam was created in the Garden of Eden, God's intention was to build His Kingdom on the earth through him. He intended for Adam to be like a glove that only functions when it is filled with the hand. Man was to be the glove whilst the Lord was to be the hand. Without the hand, a glove is just an ordinary lifeless object. This is how God intended to build His Kingdom "on earth as it is in heaven."[5]

But in Adam, this plan was aborted owing to his disobedience to God. To Adam and his descendants on earth, the earth has been cursed according to the account in Genesis.[6] Adam was a 'type' of man that did his own will and lived by the pride of his own life. He lived by his ability to "know good and evil" and through his selfish desires, the earth became corrupt and full of violence.

It was therefore necessary for Jesus Christ to come as another kind of Man to do the Father's will. He succeeded, because God was in Him and working through Him. He did nothing except

---

4 John 3:3,5
5 Matt 6:10
6 Genesis 3:17-19.

by His Father and only what He saw His Father do, so much so, that He said "If you see Me, you see the Father."[7] He was an expression of the Father, a perfect example of what it means to be in the image and likeness of God on earth and that is the kind of person to whom the earth will submit. The earth's curse was overruled for Jesus who brought peace and goodwill towards men on earth.

Out of God's love, He gave birth to the Church, which is the body of Christ. In reality, The Church is a new 'type' of Man reproduced by the impartation of the same life and Spirit of Jesus Christ into people who are descendants of Adam, thereby changing them completely into another kind of being called the 'New Man' and then training them by the Holy Spirit to live the new kind of life that Jesus Christ lived on earth. Those of us who have been well trained and renewed in our minds will be granted a place to rule and reign on earth with Christ which is the Kingdom promised to us by our Lord Jesus Christ. This change from 'Adamic' humanity to Christ humanity is called being 'born-again'.

We need to be born again to see the Kingdom of God. But, seeing the Kingdom of God is different from entering into it. The Word of God tells us that to enter we need "to be born of water and the Spirit."[8]

This can be best explained by using an example of a new born infant. For an infant to be a citizen of any earthly country, all it takes is for that baby to be born in a particular country out of parents who are from there. For us to be citizens of the Kingdom of God requires that God give birth to us, which is what happened when each of us believed in the Lord Jesus Christ. After being born of God, we become babes and need the milk of the word of God to grow, exactly as happens in the natural realm where newborn babies feed on milk in order to flourish and develop.

Babies, of course, do not remain babies, they grow up and mature. The baby may indeed be a legal citizen of the country he

---

7 John 14:9

8 John 3:5

was born in to, but to exercise authority in any area of that country, he has to earn the appropriate qualifications.

For example, one cannot just become a Bank Manager in the country of birth because one was born there; it is necessary to gain the right educational qualifications. Likewise a person cannot just have authority in the political affairs of their country of birth unless he/she has earned it by going through the required learning process and attained the other necessary qualities which will qualify them to be entrusted with political responsibility. The same applies to the Kingdom of God; we have to earn a part in the coming Kingdom of God through living out the Word of God by the Holy Spirit.

BORN OF THE SPIRIT

The statement – *'Born of the Spirit*[9] as used by the Lord means born of God because we know that God is a Spirit[10] and the Lord is the Spirit.[11] When we are born of God we become born again, making us members of the household of God, and citizens of heaven, seated in the heavenly places in Christ, and overcomers of the world.[12] It is all by His grace.

This happened to us when we believed in the finished work of Christ for us, believing that He died for our sins and we confessed Him as Lord from the heart *(Romans 10 vs 9-10).*

But after this experience, we all as believers did not immediately come to the full knowledge of who we have become, what has happened to us and even what really our purpose and future is.

Most of us only knew that our sins are forgiven and one day, we will go to heaven which is not enough to live a Christian victorious life.

---
9 John 3:6
10 John 4:24
11 Corinthians 3:17
12 1 John 3:9, 5:4-5

If we stay too long without the knowledge who we are in Christ, what has happened to us as born again children of God and what our purpose and future in Christ is, we will continue to live like mere, ordinary men which result only in a carnal way of living and this has been the state of the Church for some time.

To progress in walk with the Lord and be conformed into the image and likeness of God – thereby preparing for the kingdom of Christ to come on this earth, we need to appreciate the implication of being born of Water.

Born Of Water

To be born of water means being reproduced by the Word of God. After being born again, God expects us to "desire the sincere milk of the Word"[13] and, through our increasing knowledge of the Word of God, we will begin to recognise our new status as:

New Creations/New Man In Christ,
Member Of The Body Of Christ,
Seated In The Heavenly Places,
The Righteousness Of God In Christ,
Blessed With Every Spiritual Blessings In The Heavenly Places In Christ,
Set Free From The Law Of Sin And Death By The Law Of The Spirit Of Life In Christ Jesus,
Redeemed,
Forgiven Of Sins,
Deliverance From Sin,
Reconciled To God And To One Another,
Citizenship In Heaven
and many more.

It is these truths about the New Man – the new you in Christ - alongside many other valuable insights which we will discover when immersing ourselves in the Word of God.

---

13 1 Peter 2:2

It will not be long after learning all these great things we have in Christ, we begin to realise that we are not experiencing most of them in our lives here on earth. It will take a process for the word of God which we discover to become a reality in our lives now.

The process will convert the word of God which is Spirit[14] to water which is the Word of God used on earth to wash away the old ways of thinking, reasoning and behaving while still in the world as an old man in Adam under the influence of the evil principalities and powers in the air. The scriptures called us *"sons of disobedience"* at that time.[15]

The phrase 'born of water'- refers to the process of the Word applied in man's life on earth producing water that washes away his self exalted soul nature. It is *"the implanted word received with meekness to save his soul from all filthiness and overflow of wickedness."*[16] Water is not needed in heaven for cleansing but it performs the function of cleansing on earth. It is the word that has entered one's heart by hearing and reading that changes one here and now into the image of Christ.

The Word bears witness with the Father and the Holy Spirit in Heaven, but on earth, instead of the Word, it is the water that bears witness with the Spirit and the blood.[17] Clearly, the word in Heaven became water on earth. Christ causes His Church to be sanctified and cleansed by washing her with the water of the word.[18] Also, Jesus said in John 15:3 "You are already clean because of the word which I have spoken to you."[19]

Therefore, being born of the Spirit gets us into the Kingdom of God, but to reign and rule with Christ for a thousand years requires that we be born of water.

The process of using the Word as water to cleanse us is done by

---

14 John 6:63
15 Ephesians 5:26
16 James 1:21
17 1 John 5:7-8
18 Ephesians 5:26
19 John 15:3

the Holy Spirit through the experiences of our daily lives. This is why, as believers, we go through various trials and afflictions. It is to produce Christ. James tells us to "count it all joy when you fall into various trials, knowing that the testing of your faith produces patience. But let patience have its perfect work, that you may be perfect and complete, lacking nothing."[20]

After being *"born of God to a living hope through the resurrection of Jesus Christ from the dead"*, we are told that we still are challenged by various trials.[21] We may question this and wonder why it has to be this way? The scriptures tell us that the reason is to *"prove the genuineness of our faith which is more precious than gold which perishes."*[22] If it is precious to the Lord, it must be pleasing to Him and will glorify Him. This is why we will be rewarded for yielding to His training.

The result is the salvation of our souls which is the end of our faith. The salvation of our spirits is required for each of us to become citizens of Heaven, but to fulfil our destiny in Christ on this earth; we need the salvation of our souls. This occurs when a believer's mind is renewed by the word of God which changes his thinking, speech, actions and character.

To such humble and yielding believers, the whole of creation is waiting to be delivered from the bondage of corruption which rules them through the disobedience of the first man, Adam – an earthly man of dust.[23]

It is clear that entering into the Kingdom of God is for those who have allowed themselves to be processed by the word of God and are willing to deny themselves, take up their cross and follow the Lord Jesus Christ. The vision of the Lord for His Kingdom includes our being qualified to reign with Him in the Kingdom to come which is the next millennial reign of Christ on the earth.

This is what we are here for and every other thing we do in the

---

20 James 1:2-4
21 1 Peter 1:3-9
22 1 Peter 1:7
23 Romans 8:19

kingdom of God is an instrument used by God to prepare us for the reign of Christ on the earth. The purpose of the spiritual blessing is to make us *"holy and without blame before God in Love."*[24] Holy means to be different as God is different from all things.

We need to be aware that doing a lot of activities for the Lord, performing signs, wonders and miracles does not constitute our destiny but is a means to attaining it. Our ultimate destiny in Christ is to bear His image and be part of the overcomers who will reign with Him on earth in the millennial age. It is at this point of time that God will finally have fulfilled His original purpose for man.[25] It explains why someone like the Apostle Paul, after all the mighty deeds he had done for the Lord, still found cause to say *"I discipline my body and bring it to subjection so that after I have preached to others, I myself should not become disqualified."*[26] We may ask - from what would he be disqualified? The answer is - from the coming Kingdom of Christ on the earth - the believers' destiny.

By no means is this condemning our work for the Lord, in fact the work is necessary, because this is one of the ways in which God trains us. The work is to train our minds to be like Christ's and it is only through service that we become great in the kingdom of Christ. But it is very easy to use the work as a means of exercising authority and control over others and when that happens, we lose the opportunity to be transformed by the Holy Spirit.

Even in the body of Christ today, some have used the work they do as a means of classifying themselves above other brethren because of what they call "success".

This is why it is possible to cast out demons, prophesy and perform miracles, and yet still have the Lord say on that day *"I never knew you, depart from me, you who practice lawlessness."* [27]

---

24 Ephesians 1:4
25 Genesis 1:26-28
26 1 Corinthians 9:27
27 Matthew 7:23

So yes, it is important for us to become involved in the Kingdom work allocated to each and every one of us by the Holy Spirit in our local church, but we must not make this work an end in itself. We should appreciate that the Lord wants to use this work as a way of developing Christ in us and getting us ready to meet Him with glory at the Judgement Seat of Christ.[28]

Since the fall of Adam, right through to this present time, the whole of creation has been in bondage and pain, groaning for the revealing of another kind of Man, those called 'sons of God', who will release it from the bondage of the corruption it has been subjected to.

May I emphasis the word sons and not children of God. Sons start as children but grow up from children to sons and as sons, they handle responsibilities in the kingdom of God to build the church with Christ and ensure unity among the brethren. They are the peace makers in the kingdom of God now. They have accepted their responsibility as ministers of reconciliation.

Children are members of the family who only care for themselves and nothing else. They are not even aware if things are going right or wrong in the kingdom.

One man caused the whole creation to be put into bondage. Likewise, one Man will bring about its liberation.[29] The Man who will liberate creation is Christ Himself. It will be He, together with the overcoming saints who are taking the time to learn the lifestyle of Christ, based on self-denial. Those who, through the Word of God, and the guidance of the Holy Spirit, are repenting and being transformed in the way they think reason and behave.

Just as Adam's body belonged to him in the Garden of Eden, Christ's whole body are His today. However, when it was time for God to give Adam a helper, with whom to exercise authority over creation (his wife), God removed his rib – the place close to his heart.

---

28 Romans 8:29, Ephesians 1:5-6
29 Romans 8:19-22

Likewise with Christ, not all of His body will qualify to reign with Him on earth, but only His rib which means those who:

are close to His heart,

who are working towards God's ultimate purpose - that Christ be all and in all,

have come to know that in Christ, they are crucified with Him, died with Him, buried with Him, raised with Him, ascended with Him and enthroned with Him as members of His body and no longer themselves.

know the reality of becoming new men in Christ and living as strangers and pilgrims on this earth.

Those who are practicing the new man – they who no longer refer to themselves or to others in the body of Christ as black, white, African, European, top or low class etc, but are counting all that as rubbish in order to gain Christ, growing in the excellent knowledge of the Lord Jesus Christ.

are so much like Christ in spirit, soul and body that they are called the overcomers.

Adam said of his wife "This is flesh of my flesh and bone of my bone"[30] meaning she was just like Him in image and likeness. So it will be with Christ in the future when we shall all stand before Him at the Judgement Seat of Christ; He will say to the overcomers, you are flesh of My flesh and bone of My bone.[31] But to the rest, who were pre-occupied with this world, He will say "Away from Me." They will not lose their salvation but sadly they will not fulfil their ultimate destiny, which is to finally fulfil Gen 1:26-28 on the earth.

---

30 Genesis 2:23
31 Ephesians 5:31-33

The True Spiritual Blessing

Chapter Two

ADAM'S ORIGINAL PURPOSE

God's original purpose for man in Adam was to set up the kingdom of God on earth, so He made him in His image and likeness. But the fall of Adam disqualified him and his descendants from building the kingdom of God on earth.

Because of the fall, he was converted from the image of God to 'flesh' and 'dust' as God said, "Dust you are and to dust you shall return."[32] God also said "My Spirit shall not strive with man forever, for he is indeed flesh."[33] Now in the beginning, God said *"Let us make man in our image and according to our likeness",* and then let them have dominion. He did not say 'Let us make man in flesh and Dust to have dominion on earth. Therefore, from the moment man became flesh and dust through his fall, he lost the ability and position to exercise dominion on the earth and there was a need for another kind of Man, one who would be in the image and likeness of God to exercise dominion on the earth as the earth had been programmed to be dominated only by man who was in the image and likeness of God, or else, the word of God in Genesis 1:26-28, which is according to His eternal counsel will remain unfulfilled and leave His word void.

It was fulfilled through the coming of the Lord Jesus Christ, His crucifixion, death, burial, resurrection and ascension. The cross of Christ was the means by which God brought forth the Man in

---
32 Genesis 3:19
33 Genesis 6:3

His image and likeness —the only Man God ever testified of as "My beloved Son in whom I am well pleased."[34]

The purpose of the cross is to bring an end to the old man in Adam, a man of flesh and dust, and bring forth another kind of Man called Christ, a Man born of God in the image and likeness of God, with the ability and position to bring into fulfilment Genesis 1:26-28. And glory to God, He achieved it and said "it is finished."

So now as Adam, the fallen man, multiplies and fills the earth with his descendants through reproduction, Christ Jesus is also multiplying and filling the earth through the new birth experience by the Holy Spirit in the church. These new descendants of God, through Christ, are being trained and prepared to exercise authority over the earth with Christ as they are moulded into the image of Christ for the next millennial Kingdom of Christ on the earth.

We may ask 'Has God achieved His original purpose for man to have dominion on earth according to Genesis 1vs 26-28?' The answer clearly is NO. But it will not remain NO because the word of God cannot fail. We may wonder how it will be fulfilled. The answer is through another Man who is in the image of God – the one new man, which is Christ and the overcoming saints.

The kingdom of God that Adam failed to establish on earth is what Christ and His overcomers will fulfil in the 1000 years millennial reign.

Most believers do not appreciate it now. However, when we stand at the judgement seat of Christ, our eyes shall be opened and then only those things that are done presently in the mortal body which are of Christ by the Holy Spirit will count. That is why we will hear Jesus talk about entering into the Kingdom of God. It is the Kingdom of God on the earth, prepared for those who have been conformed to the image of Christ, who will fulfil the real destiny of man on earth. Paul had the revelation of grace but yet he said "I discipline my body and bring it into subjection,

---

34 Matthew 3: 17; 17:5

lest when I have preached to others, I myself should become disqualified."[35]

No believer would wish to be disqualified from his real destiny to reign with Christ on the earth, prepared for those who reflect the image of Christ.[36] According to Matthew 20 verses 20-28.

Brothers and sisters in Christ let us all be aware that the temptations of this world and the systems of this world are in conflict with God's plan. [37]This can make life very difficult for believers but we can take heart by the example of Paul who did not claim to be perfect but kept pressing in and forgetting those things behind him.[38] So to overcome and really be conformed to the image of Christ, we will need to deny ourselves and take up our cross and press into what Christ has achieved for us in identity, character and authority. We can thus understand why Jesus said *"Blessed are the poor in spirit; blessed are those who mourn; blessed are the merciful..."*

The whole of creation is waiting for the revealing of the sons of God who are another kind of humanity who look to Christ as their head. Creation is not waiting for the man of flesh. The man of flesh – the present sinful humanity in Adam, has inhabited the earth for over 6,000 years, since the fall of Adam and instead exercising dominion on this earth, the creation has rather controlled them and reacted harshly to his presence with such things as bad weather conditions, earthquakes, famine, discord and disease.

There is a great need for the New Man in Christ, so that the plan and purpose of God can be fulfilled on the earth. In Christ's body, the Church (which is the one new man), there is neither Greek nor Jew, black nor white, circumcised nor uncircumcised, barbarian, Scythian, slave nor free, high class nor low class but Christ is all and in all.[39] All earthly divisions of race, tribe, tongue, na-

---

35 1 Corinthians 9:27
36 Matthew 20:20-28
37 Psalm 2:1-4
38 Philippians 3:12-14
39 Colossians 3:11; Galatians 3:28

tion, cultures, traditions and religions will not and cannot stand — they will all be shaken and removed.

As true believers in Christ it should be our fervent desire to be amongst the overcoming saints. If this is the case, then as we study the truths contained in this book pray that the Holy Spirit will guide us to appreciate just how much the list of qualities mentioned in Matthew 5 are necessary in our own lives in order for us to achieve our destiny in Christ.

Chapter Three

BLESSED ARE THE POOR IN SPIRIT

"Blessed are the poor in spirit, for theirs is the kingdom of heaven."

If you are poor in anything, it is because you lack that basic necessity for living. For example, a man can be lacking in money but an animal can't, as an animal does not use money as a means of exchange. A dog can be lacking in bones to eat but a monkey couldn't be lacking in this way because most monkeys, as far as I am aware do not need bones to chew on in order to live.

A man of dust can never be poor in spirit because his spirit is dead. He is natural and of the flesh.[40] Therefore when a man is poor in spirit, it can only be possible because he is in the spirit and the spirit is part of his life. It is this which makes him different from other men –those who are dead in spirit. To be poor in spirit means that a man is alive in spirit but he is in need of more of it, because he is lacking in the things of the spirit. Therefore he is always seeking more of the spirit. This is a significant quality in those who are born again.

Before Paul encountered the Lord Jesus Christ, he said, he was blameless concerning righteousness of the law. But years later, he encountered the Lord Jesus, was converted and became born again. He describes the inner conflict he began to experience: "what I am doing, I do not understand. The evil I hate that I do

---

40 1 Corinthians 2:14-15; John 3:6

but the good I want to do, I do not do."[41] Clearly he is hungry and thirsty for that which had never appealed to him before.

The explanation is simple. When we are born again, we suddenly begin to see a kingdom which we have never seen before. This is the Kingdom of God.[42] However, seeing the Kingdom of God is quite different from entering the Kingdom of God. This seeing creates an awareness that we belong to another kingdom which is far better than this world. But initially when we attempt to live by the Kingdom of God, we find that there is a struggle to live according to the Kingdom principles. No-one has the natural ability to live the way God intended. The result will be a sense of inadequacy as Paul himself experienced. This is what it means to be poor in spirit. New, born-again, believers are still children in the Spirit and so have the consciousness for the need of more of the Spirit of Christ. This need of Christ in man's heart makes him poor in spirit. God promised such people that theirs is the Kingdom of Heaven. When Paul realised his need for more of the Lord Christ, he said *"O wretched (poor) man I am, who will deliver me from this body of death."*[43] The word 'Wretched' means poor.

On the other hand, it is possible to be born again, see the Kingdom of God and yet not recognise our impoverished spirit because of an overwhelming pre-occupation with materialism and the pleasures of this world. If we are of the opinion that gaining wealth and comfort in this world is proof of our right standing with God, we will be satisfied falsely with our spiritual walk with God and not desire more of Christ. Our lack of poverty of spirit will deprive us of the Kingdom of Heaven wherein God will exercise dominion on the earth through the overcoming saints in Christ. It is those who have learnt to put on the new man in Christ and live by the ways of the cross who will express the Kingdom of Heaven on the earth. It is those saints, with the Lord Jesus Christ as their head, who will rule and reign for a thousand years on this earth.

---

41 Romans 7:15-22
42 John 3:3
43 Romans 7:24

The church of Laodicea was an example of those who take materialism and pleasures in this world as a sign of being right with God.

The church of the Laodiceans had a lot of material and financial resources which they thought had resulted from their pleasing God. They even said *"I am rich, have become wealthy and have need of nothing"*[44] which is a sign of self- satisfaction and self confidence. This led to their spiritual condition of being 'lukewarm' and deprived them of spiritual hunger towards the Lord. Unknown to them, they were *"wretched, miserable, poor, blind and naked"*[45] in the sight of the Lord. He who will judge the living and the dead . There is nothing wrong with financial prosperity on this earth, but we must ensure we keep our fellowship with the Lord and not let wealth and material comfort deprive us of the blessing of being poor in spirit and hungering for more of the Lord Christ.

Rich believers are encouraged to glory in their humiliation.[46] They are commanded not to turn a blind eye towards the needy in the church.[47] Indeed, all believers, whether rich or poor materially, gain benefit from being poor in spirit.

---

44 Revelation 3:17
45 Revelation 3:17
46 James 1:10
47 1 John 3:17

The True Spiritual Blessing

Chapter Four

BLESSED ARE THOSE WHO MOURN

"Blessed are those who mourn for they will be comforted."

The believer who suddenly sees the Kingdom of God after the new birth becomes poor in spirit and develops a longing to be rich in the spirit. It would not be long before he realises that to be rich in spirit comes at a price. The price is self-denial. Remember the words of our Lord Jesus Christ: *"If anyone desires to come after Me, let him deny himself, take up his cross daily and follow Me."*[48]

Even when believers engage in self-denial, their rate of growth to richness in Christ will usually not be at the speed they expect and this will lead to mourning. You see His ways are not our ways, His thoughts are not our thoughts[49] and likewise, His timing is not our timing.

We will mourn because after doing the things we thought were necessary for us to do in order to experience the riches of Christ in the Spirit; we will not always experience immediate rewards. At this point we may become discouraged and wish to turn back to how our life used to be, or we will begin to mourn. Mourning involves continual prayer and seeking the Lord for answers in His word.

Paul had a similar experience when he was afflicted with an in-

---
48 Luke 9:23
49 Isaiah 55:8

firmity and on three occasions he sought the Lord regarding the matter.[50] The Lord responded with an answer that caused him to rejoice in his infirmities, reproaches and weaknesses. It is possible to imagine Paul mourning and beseeching the Lord by saying 'Lord you said in your word that I am healed by your stripes, why then should I have this infirmity?'

But the Lord's answer so strengthened Paul that the adversary, Satan could no longer discourage him by physical affliction because the Lord said to him *"My grace is sufficient for you and My strength is made perfect in your weakness."*[51] So Paul knew from that day, that as much as he would prefer not to have his weakness, it was a way for the Lord to work through him and be glorified in the process, because the Lord told him that His strength is made perfect in Paul's weakness.

Paul could have been discouraged like others and turned back, but he would have missed the revelation of the Lord Jesus Christ who revealed the secret to him that *"all things work together for good to them that love Him and are called according to His purpose."*[52] Even in weakness he knew he was still more than a conqueror because the Lord's strength would work through him. It is impossible to discourage a believer who has this attitude. Nothing can separate the believer from the love of Christ.

We are admonished to pray always and not lose heart.[53] This is because it is possible to lose heart after praying when answers do not come as quickly as we would like. As we mourn and persevere in prayer, the Lord will comfort us.

The letter to the Hebrews encourages us *"do not cast away your confidence, which has great reward. For you need endurance, so that after you have done the will of God, you may receive the promise."*[54] Jesus said if you put your hand on the plough and look back, you are not fit for the kingdom of heaven.[55] In other words,

---

50 2 Corinthians 12:7-9
51 2 Corinthians 12:9
52 Romans 8:28
53 Luke 18:1
54 Hebrews 10:35-36
55 Luke 9:62

if we make a commitment to the things of Christ and later back out, we disqualify ourselves from the Kingdom.

Looking back only happens because we fail to see the rewards we expect within a reasonable time. It may some times result in discouragement and a compromising of commitment. This is called unfaithfulness which does not reflect God's character. God is a faithful God and so, as His children, born again in His image and likeness, we too must be faithful. The Lord Jesus Christ will only reward us at the judgement seat if we are good and faithful. He says *"Be faithful until death, and I will give you the Crown of Life."*[56]

Saints of God, every true overcomer in the kingdom of Christ will go through this kind of discouragement, but if we determine to remain faithful and press on despite the discouragement, we will find ourselves mourning before the Lord. We will have doubts and questions which the Lord already has answers for by the Holy Spirit as was the case with Paul (explained above.) Remember the Holy Spirit is called the Comforter.

As we mourn before the Lord, the Holy Spirit will comfort us by answering the questions of our hearts which will bring us into revelations of the Lord Jesus Christ, increase our faith and impart the patience of Christ in us. Thus will we find ourselves becoming more like Christ.

This is also what it means to *"learn Christ"* [57] The good news is that the mourning is a sign that we are truly blessed with the spiritual blessing of possessing a new kind of life which is in Christ called *Zoe* (a life different from physical life – God's kind of life) and also that we are growing into maturity to become the 'sons' for whom creation has been waiting.

In the next millennial age, when the Kingdom of Christ shall be established on earth and Christ will rule for a thousand years, only the overcomers will rule with Him. It is at these times that our destiny as mankind in God's agenda will be fulfilled. If we qualify,

---
56 Revelation 2:10
57 Ephesians 4:20

we will fulfil that ultimate destiny. But, if we fail to qualify, we will suffer loss with much weeping and regret.

This present evil age is only a training ground for us. All we are doing now is to be trained, to pass our spiritual examinations and be qualified for the future manifestation of the Kingdom of Christ on this earth.[58] At this moment, we are strangers and pilgrims on this earth, groaning and mourning because we have a different spirit and life which is the Spirit and Life of the Almighty God in Christ Jesus. We must also realise that the spirit of this world which is the same spirit working in the mortal body/flesh of man, belongs to the adversary and so fights against the Spirit of Christ residing in our spirit. Therefore in choosing to yield to the Spirit of Christ within us, we must also choose to ignore the desires in our bodies when they contradict the will of God. Resisting our flesh also leads to mourning but serves to align us with the perfect will of God.

Many of us in Christ today do not appreciate this blessing,[59] but we see it as a problem and it sometimes causes us to be angry with the Lord. The mourning is because of the life and Spirit of God in you, which is working in you things that are producing the glory of God in you. The nature of the Spirit and life in you in Christ Jesus stands in opposition to the spirit of this world. The nature of your flesh is accustomed to living its own way, but when the Spirit of Christ comes into you, He will prompt you to do the will of God. It is His desire that you complete the will of God for your life.[60]

By no means do I wish to affirm ungodly suffering that some in the body of Christ have said is from God. Suffering like poverty, sickness and diseases are not of God and a believer must not accept them but reject them with the word of God. Jesus suffered poverty on the cross so that we would not be poor; Jesus was afflicted with stripes on His body for our healing. We must always distinguish between illegitimate mourning which comes from ungodly suffering and legitimate mourning which results from the chastening of the Lord[61] to help us become more Christ-like.

---

58 Acts 14:22, 1Corinthians 9:24-27, 2Peter 1:5-10
59 2 Corinthians 4:17-18
60 John 4:34
61 Hebrews 12:5-11

Chapter Five

Blessed Are the Meek

"Blessed are the meek for they shall inherit the earth."

Through the blessing of mourning and being comforted by the Holy Spirit[62], the believer will realise more and more how powerless he is to do God's will without Christ. He will appreciate that he is a branch while the Lord is the Vine who supplies the required life for living in the will of God. He will begin to depend on the Lord's help and will seek the Lord's help all the time.

Like Paul, he will know that His *"grace is sufficient"* for him.[63] You will appreciate His grace more and know that His Strength can only be perfected in believers weakness. You are always drawn to the throne of grace – the place of prayer, intimacy and worship.

The knowledge of the will of God and doing it will become like precious gold to the believer. His entire being will always be crying out *"not my will but yours be done."*[64]

The meek are those who have come to realise that the purpose of their living in this world is to do the will of God, which is not what they would like to do naturally. But after being baptised into Christ and going through the chastening of God by the Holy Spir-

---
62 Romans 8:26
63 2 Corinthians 12:9
64 Luke 22:42

it, they have been 'broken' and come to realise that their will and desire is of no eternal value. Hence, they have acquired a new vision and desire to do the will of God, which is the only thing anyone can do in this world for any eternal value. Because of this kind of mindset, they begin to *"lay up treasures in heaven."*

Meekness is the virtue that all the heroes of faith[65] in the scriptures possessed and it enabled them to walk with God to the point that their faith impressed God and He acknowledged them in His Word. We cannot overcome evil with evil, only with good. Pride is commonplace in this world and the only way to conquer pride is through meekness (humility) toward God and others. Meekness is doing the will of God in His way and not our own way. As we become meek, we develop a desire to do the will of God as explained above. However, there is more for each of us to learn before we can do the will of God. For instance, we may have a desire to cure every sick person in our neighbourhood which is a noble ambition, but to live this desire out will necessitate acquiring the identity of a medical doctor which can only be achieved by attending medical school and studying for many years.

Likewise, the same principle goes with doing the will of God. Just as sick people are cured by Medical Doctors and if anyone desires to cure sick people, he or she would have to first become a Medical Doctor, in the kingdom of God, doing the will of God is done by Christ because He is the only one who possess the ability to do the will of God and if a believers desires to do the will of God (which must be the desire of every true born again child of God), he or she must first become Christ, which happened through the new birth.

The next thing is to learn Christ and put Him on daily. This involves learning to think, speak and act like Him. It is called repenting. A born babe in Christ starts the learning process by first having a desire for the sincere milk of the word of God and as such believers grow and have their mind renewed, they will have more ability to do the will of God and then advance into partaking of the solid meat of the word of God. The outcome is that they will be more obedient to God, in other word, they become increasingly meek.

---

65 Hebrews 11

Learning Christ

Christ can be taught and learned in the school of the Holy Spirit. You may ask — what is the school of the Holy Spirit? For the children of Israel, it was the wilderness journey on the way to the Promised Land; for the present-day believer in Christ, it is the experiences we have in this evil world. The believer is coached by the Holy Spirit in the Church through the Apostles, Prophets, Evangelists, Pastors and Teachers.

In Ephesians 4:8-13, the Lord descended and ascended far above the heavens because He wants to fill all things, meaning all things expressing His Fathers will.To accomplish this task, He appointed the Apostles, Prophets, Evangelist, Pastors and Teachers whose assignment is to love Him so much as spending time with Him to know Him and be filled by Him, so that they can go and reveal what they have seen of Him to the saints in the church until all the saints come to the measure of the full stature of Christ. Full measure of the Stature of Christ is the image and likeness of Him.

The fivefold ministries in the Church will have to reveal to the believers:

The new identity in Christ; authority of the new identity; inheritance of the new identity; character of the new identity; responsibilities of the new identity on earth; future and hope of the new identity and more that cannot be explained in this book. I will only briefly mention the identity of the believer in Christ because of the subject of this book.

What is the identity of the new man in Christ? He is:

Born Of God And Does Not Sin,

A Heavenly Citizen,

Cleansed By The Word

Justified

Glorified

Sanctified

Righteous

Blessed With Every Spiritual Blessing

Subject To The Law Of The Spirit Of Life In Christ Jesus

An Overcomer Of The World By Faith

Holy As God Is Holy

A Chosen Generation, Royal Priesthood, Holy Nation, God's Special People

Complete In Christ Who Is The Head Of All Principality and Power.

In the identity of the new man in Christ, there are no Jew, no Gentile, no Black, no white, no African, no European, no upper class, no lower class, no male, no female, etc.[66] The new man is an entirely new creation given birth by God Himself through the resurrection of Jesus Christ from the dead.[67] Since the believer is born of God, God is his Father and his identity is God's identity just as Jesus Christ who is the image and the expression of God said, 'I am from above and not of this world'. As we put on this new man in Christ, the abilities of Christ will become ours and we will begin to spontaneously yield to the will of God. We will share Christ's ambition when He said *"My food is to do the will of Him who sent Me and to finish His work."*[68]

This is true meekness or humility and the promise to the meek is that they will inherit the earth. The whole creation is waiting for the revealing of the meek (sons of God) who have put on Christ, the new man – these are sons of God through faith in Christ Jesus.

---

66 Ephesians 4:22-24
67 1 Peter 1:1-3
68 John 4:34

Through meekness, the believer in Christ will see that all he has gained in the flesh is rubbish including his old identity in terms of his race, culture, gender, religious background, family heritage and class in society. All these will become insignificant to him. He will begin to seek to put on his new identity in Christ called the New man.

At this stage, he enjoys the blessing of meekness where the earth now begins to yield to his instruction. The entire creation that has been *"eagerly waiting for the manifestation of the sons of God"*[69] will recognise him as a Son of God and all the elements will submit to him.[70]

The heart of the meek desires to do the will of God and also to be who God, in His word, has declared him to be in Christ Jesus - a new man, regardless what persecutions may arise from those in the world or in the Church who still have confidence in and indulge in their old Adamic identities. For example, they still refer to themselves as black brothers, white brothers, African churches, Nigerian churches, British churches, Indian churches, white pastors etc. These 'fleshly' ways of speaking hinders growth in the body of Christ.

The meek will express the Lord's nature because they are no longer living for themselves as they come to know that they are crucified, dead and buried with Christ and in resurrection, they were raised with Christ as a new man in whom is Christ living in and through them. They will be expressing the image and likeness of God and therefore qualify to inherit the earth which has been programmed by the word of God to be controlled by people in the image and likeness of God. They have fully identified themselves with Christ in death and resurrection and hence focus their minds above to where Christ is sitting at the right hand of God. This makes them spiritual people who now worship God in the spirit and have lost all confidence in the flesh. We can only lose confidence in something that has disappointed us because it has proven to be inadequate. This is what Jeremiah meant when he said *"O LORD, my strength, and my fortress, and my refuge in*

---

69 Romans 8:19
70 Galatians 4:1-4

the day of affliction, the Gentiles shall come unto thee from the ends of the earth, and shall say, Surely our fathers have inherited lies, vanity, and things wherein there is no profit. Shall a man make gods unto himself, and they are no gods? Therefore, behold, I will this once cause them to know, I will cause them to know mine hand and my might; and they shall know that my name is The LORD."[71] The worthlessness of the flesh comes to us through its disappointments and failures. This will cause us to mourn but the blessed Holy Spirit being our comforter will comfort at the same time. After losing confidence in ourselves and experiencing the worthlessness of our flesh, then we will share Paul's agonising plea *"O wretched man that I am. Who will deliver me from the body of death?"*[72]

---

71 Jeremiah 16:19-21
72 Romans 7:24

Chapter Six

Blessed Are Those Who Hunger And Thirst For Righteousness

Righteousness is defined as right standing with God. Right standing with God means that we can stand in His presence without condemnation because God accepts us and we are pleasing to Him in Christ Jesus. We know that *"all have sinned and fallen short of the glory of God"*[73], It is the 'natural man', who has the Adamic nature where sin first originated in man, who cannot stand before God because he is not righteous before God.

We see the evidence of sin, after the fall of Adam when God was approaching him and his wife in the Garden of Eden. We are told that they hid themselves away from the presence of God while God was looking for them as was His custom in the cool of the day. Why was Adam hiding away from God? It was because his sin converted him into another kind of man, one who was unrighteous before God. This self-consciousness of his unrighteousness produced fear in Adam and it was this fear that drew him away from the Lord.

This is the kind of man that Adam reproduced on the earth who inhabits the world today. We can see why the natural man cannot come to God by himself and cannot know spiritual things. Since the fall, the 'natural man 'has become unrighteous before God and everything he has done is unrighteous before the Lord. Jesus Christ said that *"a good tree bears good fruit and a bad tree bears*

---

73 Romans 3:23

bad fruit." The good tree cannot bear bad fruit neither can bad trees bear good fruit. It therefore follows that all that has come from the natural man is not righteous in God's eyes. Unrighteousness includes classifications of race, culture, religion, nationality, tribe and language.

Since the fall of Adam there has only been one man who lived in this world who has been accepted by God as righteous — the Man Jesus Christ, the Son of the Living God. Unlike Adam who was "created" by God, Jesus Christ was "born" of God, so the exact life and nature of His Father God was reproduced in Him at birth. During the first thirty years of His life in this world, Our Lord was tested and tempted to act unrighteously, yet He did not sin, but continued to be righteous before God. He was subject to the laws of God given to Moses and obeyed them all without sin. Following all his trials, God confirmed Him as righteous by declaring:

"This is My beloved Son in whom I am well pleased."

Just as through Adam, the unrighteous natural man has populated the earth by reproduction, through Christ Jesus, another kind of Man is being reproduced on the earth. This is a righteous kind of Man in Christ called the New Man in Christ. The church is made up of such people who are righteous not by virtue of their actions but because they are born of God. As such, they have the same life and nature as God through Christ Jesus. This is why the word 'born again' is used to describe them. They were once born into this world naturally but later were born again spiritually into the kingdom of God. The Church is also called the Body of Christ. Since it is the Body of Christ, its identity can only be from Christ Himself, the only righteous Man according to God's standard.

Everyone who is born again in Christ Jesus is considered *"a new creation, old things have passed away, behold all things are new."*[74] The old things which have passed away are all the unrighteous things of the natural man, so the person who is born again will suddenly become hungry and thirsty for another way of living because of the new, righteous nature he has received in

---

74 2 Corinthians 5:17

Christ Jesus. This hunger and thirst manifests itself as a desire to experience the righteousness which has been imparted to them by the regeneration of the spiritman in Christ Jesus.

So as a new man in Christ, we become righteous and holy persons objectively. However, subjectively, we do not come close to acting righteously. The Holy Spirit working in us will convict us about those actions that are not right in God's sight, and we will hunger and thirst for righteousness. As this experience continues, we find ourselves becoming more aware that we are strangers and pilgrims on this earth and, like Abraham; we begin to desire a heavenly country.

Paul counted all that he had gained in the flesh as rubbish. The flesh refers to our old nature — who we used to be in the world before becoming a new men in Christ. The flesh is our former identity in the world but now in Christ we are crucified and dead and Christ is the one who now lives in us. Our former identities in the world were unrighteous. Only that which is Christ in us is righteous. Therefore, we gain Christ by counting as rubbish our former identities and classifications in the world. We are not of the world as Christ is not of the world.

The transformation is not an easy one but it is facilitated by our hunger and thirst for righteousness. This desire produces the motivation in us to embrace our new identity in Christ despite the suffering and persecution we may encounter. This will shape each of us more into His image and as we are conformed to His image, we will exercise dominion on earth; this, dear brethren, sounds like a real blessing to me. What greater blessing can a believer enjoy than that all things on earth become subject to him or her? The believers in Christ who are blessed with this thirst and hunger for righteousness have come to know that they are made righteous in Christ through the finished work of His cross. Although, at this present time, we may not have experienced this righteousness on earth because we have not allowed Christ to dwell sufficiently in our souls. So we find ourselves hungering for more of Christ, in order to express the righteousness of God which we have received by faith in the Lord Jesus Christ.

We should always pray the prayers of the Spirit *"to be strengthened with might through His spirit in the inner man..."*[75] and that we be *"filled with the knowledge of His will in all wisdom and spiritual understanding...."*[76]

Satisfying The Thirst And Hunger

As we all know, to quench thirst, we drink water and to satisfy hunger, we eat. Believers must crave the Word of God more than physical food.[77] When we are thirsty and hungry for righteousness, we are really thirsty and hungry for a Person who is the Lord Jesus Christ Himself. Scripture tells us that Christ *"became for us wisdom from God and of righteousness, sanctification and redemption."*[78] Jeremiah prophesied Jesus' coming on earth with the words:

"In those days and at that time, I will cause to grow up to David a branch of righteousness, He shall execute judgement and righteousness in the earth. In those days, Judah will be saved and Jerusalem will dwell safely and this is the name by which she will be called **THE LORD OUR RIGHTEOUSNESS.**"[79]

The Lord Himself is our righteousness. So to quench our thirst and satisfy our hunger for righteousness, we need to feed on Him through His word and drink of Him through prayer. How is that possible? He said *"As the living Father sent Me and I live because of My Father so he that feeds on Me shall live because of Me."*[80] He also said *"I am the living bread which came down from heaven. If anyone eats of this bread, he will live forever and the bread that I shall give is My flesh which I shall give for the life of the world."*[81] Jesus further added *"unless you eat the flesh of the Son of Man and drink His blood, you have no life in you. Whoever*

---

75 Ephesians 3:16-19
76 Colossians 1:9-11
77 Jeremiah 23:12
78 1 Corinthians 1:30
79 Jeremiah 33:15-16
80 John 6:57
81 John 6:51

eats My flesh and drinks My blood has eternal life and I will raise him up at the last day. For My flesh is food indeed and My blood is drink indeed. He who eats My flesh and drinks My blood abides in Me and I in him."[82]

So we have to eat and drink the Lord.How do we do this? The Lord is the Word.[83] (In the beginning was the Word and the Word was with God and the Word was God). Therefore we eat and drink the Lord by reading, meditating and confessing the Word of God. We cannot separate the Lord from His word, they are One.[84]

John 6:27 – Do not labour for the food that perishes, but for the food which endures to everlasting life, which the Son of Man will give you, because the Father has set His seal on Him.

From the scripture above, there are two kinds of food –

First is the food that perishes, which is the physical food that men eat for the nourishment of the body. This is what the natural man lives his life for. In Genesis 3:17-19, the natural man was cursed to toil and sweat before eating this food that perishes. Jesus said man should not worry about his life in Matthew 6:25-33, and what did Jesus call his life? what to eat, what to drink and what to wear. So what to eat is part of what makes the life of the natural man. In the wilderness, God tested the children of Israel to let them know that man shall not live by bread alone but by every word that proceeds out of the mouth of God. The food that perish is the bread that the natural man lives by.

The other kind of food mention in John 6:27 is the food that does not perish but endures to everlasting life. Anything that has everlasting life in it definitely has the Lord in it because everlasting life belongs to God alone, it is a God kind of life as the word of God says in John 1:4, In Him was life and the life was the light of men. Life is only in Christ and if anyone wants life, he or she would have to be in Him.

---

82 John 6:53-55
83 John 1:1
84 John 5:39

What kind of food is this?

Jesus said I am the bread of life. Bread is food and life is from everlasting life, therefore Jesus Christ is the food that endures to everlasting life and it will only take Him to give this food.

How can we come in contact with Him as food since He is in heaven with the Father?

Remember who He is in John 1:1 – *"In the beginning was the word and the word was with God and the word was God"*.

So the word is God and God is the word. This is further confirmed in Revelation 19:13 – *"He was clothed with a robe dipped in blood, and His name is called THE WORD OF GOD."*

The word which is God is what became flesh in John 1:14. So the flesh of Jesus Christ is the word, therefore if we can eat His flesh and drink His blood as the life of the flesh is in the blood, we will be eating and drinking the Lord Himself.

Conclusively, if we eat the word of God, we will be eating the Lord. No wonder we are instructed by the Lord in Joshsua 1:8 and Psalm 1:1-3, to meditate on the word of God day and night to bear fruit, be prosperous and have success.

How do we eat the Lord, who is the Word?

We eat and drink the Lord by reading the word but more than reading, we also pray the word of God.

Let me give this encouragement first. The human body is fed by food because the body has the same life as the food. Why? They both came from the same place and that is the ground and are both dust. Therefore if as believers the Lord is telling us to feed on Him, the real life and nature of the believer is the Lord Himself. We are made of the Lord, we are God's workmanship created in Christ Jesus(Ephesians 2:10). This is confirmed in 1Corinthains 6:17 – *"He that is joined to the Lord is One Spirit with Him"*; ….also in 1John 4:17 – *"as He is so are we in this world"*.

We have been born again of the incorruptible word of God which lives and abides forever as revealed in 1Peter 1:23. So if we are born of the word, we are the word in our spiritman. This is why we can be confident to look at the scriptures as say *"it is written of me"*, just as Jesus also spoke.

EATING THE LORD JESUS CHRIST BY THE WORD OF GOD

We start to eat the Lord by reading the word of God in the bible diligently and consistently.

Realise that the Holy Spirit is the teacher of the word of God and not man's ability to understand.

When the word of God is read, it immediately feeds the mind but does not feed the believer in the mind, it has to get into the spirit of the believer.

The word of God in the mind needs to be understood by the believer and the understanding will only come from the Lord. The good news is that the understanding required is already given by the Lord, we only need to exercise the understanding we have in Christ Jesus.

1John 5:20 – *"And we know that the Son of God has come and has given us an undertstanding thatwe might know Him who is true and that are in Him who is true, in His Son Jesus Christ. This is the true God and eternal life".*

The Son of God has (past tense) given us ....

The understanding we have used is by the Holy Spirit to teach us the word of God. The Holy Spirit does it line upon line,precept upon precept (Isaiah 28:). We cannot understand the word ourselves, so whatever we understand from the word of God when we read, is what we need for feed our spirit at the time and there should be no striving to know a lot all at once, or else it will puff up the believer.

To feed the spirit, we simply pray with the word of God that we understand from the Holy Spirit. Also remember as explain before that the word of God is the Lord Himself. So when praying with the word, we cannot separate it from the Lord.

For example, if a believer read from the word of God that we must love one another, as Jesus Christ has loved us, we must love one another or he or she reads in the word of God that we must love our enemies and bless those who curse us..

The believer must realise that without the Lord, we can do nothing and that God is love. So when praying, he or she should pray by praising the Lord that He alone is love and thanking Him that He has made the believer one spirit with Himself through the death and resurrection of Christ. Therefore ask the Lord to fill him so much in his heart and love other believers through him, love the enemies through him.

Samples of Praying the word is in *APPENDIX A* of this book where we can see practically how the understanding of the word of God given us by the Holy Spirit is converted to prayer. Please do not take it as a formula to be used, but let the Holy Spirit use it to teach and lead in praying in the Spirit. It is called praying in the spirit with the understanding; there is also praying in the spirit with the spirit also, which we do by praying in tongues. I will encourage that a lot.

Come To Me – For The Hunger

John 6:35, "He who comes to Me shall never hunger, and he who believes in Me shall never thirst"

From the scripture above those who are hungry are fed by coming to the Lord Jesus Christ, as He said in John 6:35, *"He who comes to Me shall never hunger"*

In Matthew 11:28, the call to come to the Lord is to those who labour and are heavy laden.

Man never had to labour until the fall of Adam, the first man in the garden of Eden. After the fall, the ground was cursed for the sake of man and from that moment, he had to toil (labour) and sweat to eat, which became a heavy burden on mankind as they were dominated by the law of sin and death – (a kind of mankind called Adamic race). This applied only to the Adamic race because God said ''Cursed is the ground for your sake''......, Adam's sake and all his descendants born of him which includes all the human race in this world without Christ, because it is written in the scriptures, '' in Adam all died''…..1Corinthians 15:22; also therefore, just as through one man sin entered the world, and death through sin, and thus death spread to all men, because all sinned'' – Romans 5:12

When Christ said *"come unto Me all you that labour and heavy laden"*, it was a call to the entire Adamic descendants to come out of every tribe, people, nation and tongue formed on earth from the fall of Adam by reproduction, into His own new Humanity, the Church, the one new Man, where the law of the Spirit of life operates. The crossover into the new Humanity in Christ is what it means to come to the Lord and that is being Born Again. At that moment, we were filled with the Spirit of the Lord and our spirit was regenerated and we experience a kind of satisfaction that we have not had before in the world. The believer from that time of conversion will experience the hunger for the Lord, a hunger he or she had not had before. It makes the believer poor in spirit as explained in chapter 3.

In 1Corinthians 12:13, the Lord described it this way, *"For by one Spirit have we all been baptised into one body (the church, one new Man) and have been made to drink of one Spirit"*.The One body there is the body of Christ.

Believe in Me – For the Thirst

For by one Spirit we were all baptized into one body—whether Jews or Greeks, whether slaves or freeand have all been made to drink into one Spirit. (1Corinthians 12:13)

These things I have written to you who believe in the name of the Son of God, that you may know that you have eternal life, and that you may continue to believe in the name of the Son of God. (1John 5:13)

And truly Jesus did many other signs in the presence of His disciples, which are not written in this book; but these are written that you may believe that Jesus is the Christ, the Son of God, and that believing you may have life in His name. (John 20:30-31) After coming to the Lord through the new birth, we then have to drink of the Spirit continually as stated in John 6:35. It entails to continue to believe in the name of the Jesus Christ and continue discovering more about Him and keep believing more and more as we keep learning of Him in order to satisfy the thirst. This is why after being born again, we are told to be filled with the Spirit. If we fail in this area, we will be born again but have challenges in living out a victorious life in Christ.

In 1Corinthians 12:13, the last part of the scripture says that we have been made to drink of one Spirit. Just like the human body which was made out of dust and the dust came out of the waters from the account of God's word in Genesis Chapter 1, hence the body cannot survive without water. It has been established as a fact that the body can survive without food for a period of time but not without water.

A man is born into this world once, but will be sustained all the days of his life by the intake of nutrients from what he or she eats and drinks. The same goes for the believers, after being born of the Spirit, we will only survive and continually live victoriously by continually being fill with the Spirit, which is drinking the One Spirit of Christ.

The promise to all those who thirst and hunger for righteousness, is that they will be filled. Their eyes will be opened to see the Lord by the Spirit of Wisdom and Revelation and this will cause their hearts to be filled with Christ by faith which comes by hearing the word of God. Then, out of the abundance of their heart which is filled with Christ, they will speak out Christ and show themselves to be in His likeness.

CHAPTER SEVEN

BLESSED ARE THE MERCIFUL

Mercy is the nature of God expressed out of His love towards those who do not deserve it. It is an act of compassion demonstrated by someone who has God's kind of life, in Christ, towards others who do not deserve it.

Mercy is something that God desires to express. He is not grudgingly merciful; rather, it is His nature and desire to be merciful.[85]

When we were born again, it was out of the abundant mercy of God as revealed in 1Peter 1vs 3.

Blessed be the God and Father of our Lord Jesus Christ, who according to His abundant mercy has begotten us again to a living hope through the resurrection of Jesus Christ from the dead.[86]

In these last days, it is very important for us in Christ (who desire to please the Lord and looking to be over-comers to reign with Christ) to be merciful because the love of many will grow cold and it will take looking beyond men's negative actions towards us, to continue doing good and pleasing God. In spite of the prevalence of selfishness in the world today, we have to be merciful; doing good and so pleasing the Lord. As such, men will

---

85 Matthew 9:13
86 1Peter1:3

see our good works and glorify the Father in heaven.

Before mercy can be truly demonstrated, the heart must first be full of love as revealed in the Ephesians 2 vs1-7, where God has demonstrated an example of His love and mercy for us to emulate;

And you He made alive, who were dead in trespasses and sins, in which you once walked according to the course of this world, according to the prince of the power of the air, the spirit who now works in the sons of disobedience, among whom also we all once conducted ourselves in the lusts of our flesh, fulfilling the desires of the flesh and of the mind, and were by nature children of wrath, just as the others.[87]

But God, who is rich in mercy, because of His great love with which He loved us, even when we were dead in trespasses, made us alive together with Christ (by grace you have been saved), and raised us up together, and made us sit together in the heavenly places in Christ Jesus, that in the ages to come He might show the exceeding riches of His grace in His kindness toward us in Christ Jesus.

Before we received forgiveness of sins and were made alive together with Christ, we were all dead in trespasses and sins, living against the will of God under the influence and rule of satan, the prince of the power of the air. All we deserved then was destruction and hell. However, on account of God's great love for us, He was rich in mercy and, by this, demonstrated the act of compassion which we did not deserve, by sending His own Son as a sacrifice for our sins; making Him the sin offering for us, so that we could become His righteousness in Christ.

The result of this act of mercy from God to us is that we received the life of Christ called Eternal life, which is God's kind of life. In this life is the same ability to show mercy as God has shown to us.

---

87 Ephesians 2:1-7

Christ On The Cross

Father, forgive them, for they do not know what they do.[88]

This is a prayer made by the Lord Jesus Christ on the cross for those who crucified Him. It is a prayer of mercy for those who were undeserving of it because He was punished for what He had not done. Pilate indeed confessed before the crucifixion in Luke 23vs4 – **'I find no fault in this man.'**

I believe this prayer was necessary in order for us to be cleared of *that* sin and for the Holy Spirit to come on earth as promised by the Father.

We as believers are still living in a world that is dark and blinded to the kingdom of God. Therefore we will have to deal with people in this world (even also babes in Christ) who do not know what they do as regards transgressing the law of God. The whole world and its system is under satanic influence and, consequently, operate by the wisdom of the rulers of darkness - a wisdom that is corrupt and self centred.

As believers, if we will have to wait till people in this world are right and worthy before showing kindness, we will end up doing nothing but be full of disappointment and even anger. To be a blessing and change lives to the glory of God, we will have to be like Jesus, who prayed for the forgiveness of His murderers so that God's eternal purpose to save men and build them up to be sons, bringing them to glory, will be fulfilled.

Stephen was a man full of the faith and power of the Holy Spirit and with the Spirit, he was able to demonstrated the same mercy to those who set up false witnesses against him and stoned him to death in Acts 7vs60, where he prayed like Jesus saying, Lord, do not charge them with this sin.

He was able to do this because he was full of the Holy Spirit, by whom he had received the same eternal life we also share. As believers today, we have the same life and so, should express

---
[88] Luke 23:34

the same mercy towards those who offend us. Remember after the resurrection of Jesus Christ from the dead (John 20vs22-23), He breathed on the disciples saying, Receive the Holy Spirit. If you forgive the sins of any, they are forgiven them; if you retain the sins of any, they are retained.

At that moment, He gave us the same power to forgive sins on earth as He did in Mark 2vs10-11 and in 2Corinthians 5vs18, we have now received the ministry of Reconciliation.

With the power to forgive sins, we can release many people from the bondage of satan and exercise the power to bind and loose for the kingdom and will of God to be established on earth as it is in heaven.

The paralytic was instantly healed[89] because Jesus exercised the power to forgive sins on earth as a Son of Man. In Christ, we are in His Humanity - the One New Man - and the same power has been given to us as ministers of reconciliation. His new Humanity I say, because if anyone is in Christ, he is a new creation, old things have passed away; Behold all things have become new; hence we are exhorted by the Lord to put on the New Man who was created according to God in true righteousness and holiness.

But note that the power of forgiveness will only work through us if we, in the body of Christ, are merciful to one another and are long-suffering to one another, bearing with one another in love. How will the power of forgiveness work through us to set men free when we ourselves are not forgiving one another?

Stephen is an example to all those who have the same Holy Spirit. The same Spirit is able to overcome evil with good through believers today because He is the same yesterday, today and forever. The Lord Jesus was anointed with the Holy Spirit and power and He went about doing good and healing all those oppressed by the devil. He not only healed but also did good by the Holy Spirit and power.

---

89 Mark 2:1-12

Forgiveness Of Sins

1Timothy 1vs16: However, for this reason I obtained mercy, that in me first Jesus Christ might show all long-suffering, as a pattern to those who are going to believe on Him for everlasting life.

Mercy is a pattern and an example from the Lord to all who believe in Christ Jesus. In the parable of the good Samaritan[90], the spiritual giants of the day like the Priests and Levites passed by the needy wounded man, but the Samaritan, who only believed and held fast to the simplicity that is in Christ, ministered mercy to this needy man with what he had and he was commended by the Lord.

The Lord only wants to see Himself lived out through us, so our assignment is to present ourselves to Him as living sacrifices and feed on Him through His word, allowing the implanted word to save our souls from self and letting Him live His live in us.

In the Lord's prayer, the Lord Jesus Christ taught us to pray, 'Father forgive us as we forgive those who trespass against us.' Later in the epistles (which were written after the coming of the Holy Spirit, who is teaching us all truth and things that could not be comprehended when the Lord Jesus was on earth,) we are told that God has already forgiven us all trespasses in Christ. So as we have been forgiven in Christ, we all have to now forgive those who offend us.

Ephesians 1vs7-8:

In Him we have redemption through His blood, the forgiveness of sins, according to the riches of His grace which He made to abound toward us in all wisdom and prudence.

Colossians 3vs12-13:

Therefore, as the elect of God, holy and beloved, put on tender mercies, kindness, humility, meekness, long-suffering; bearing

---
90 Luke 10:25 - 37

with one another, and forgiving one another, if anyone has a complaint against another; even as Christ forgave you, so you also must do.

Colossians 2vs13:

And you, being dead in your trespasses and the uncircumcision of your flesh, He has made alive together with Him, having forgiven you all trespasses.

This is why, in Christ, we are justified freely by the grace of God and if through the offence of Adam, judgement came to all men resulting in condemnation, even so through the righteous act of Christ, the free gift has come to us in Christ, resulting in justification of life. If we are then justified like this, we should mercy always.

Condemnation became part of man's nature through the fall and so all men were condemned, consequently taking vengeance on one another. But in Christ, justification is part of the nature of the believer; there is no condemnation. Therefore justification is all that can be found in believers, and out of justification comes mercy which triumphs over judgement.

Reward Of The Merciful

The reward of the merciful is that they will obtain mercy. This is not limited to our present age but also at the judgement seat of Christ.

In this present age, the Lord says, 'Whatever you want men to do to you, do also to them. This is the Law and the Prophets.' So as you sow mercy in others, you also will receive mercy.

For the age to come at the judgement seat of Christ, mercy triumphs over judgement according to James 2vs13.

'The Lord grant mercy to the household of Onesiphorus,

for he often refreshed me, and was not ashamed of my chains; but when he arrived in Rome, he sought me out very zealously and found me. The Lord grant to him that he may find mercy from the Lord in that Day—and you know very well how many ways he ministered to me at Ephesus.'**[91]**

Onesiphorus showed mercy to Paul in the times of Paul's afflictions which he called 'my chains'. As a reward, Paul was inspired by the Holy Spirit to pray that Onesiphorus would receive mercy from the Lord in that Day, which is the Day of Judgement of the believers called the Judgement seat of Christ (2Corinthians 5vs10). The mercy we show others today will be rewarded at the presence of the Lord on the day of judgement.

In Luke 14vs12-14, the Lord Jesus Christ revealed an eternal wisdom which, if applied, will be deserving of reward both now and in the age to come. He said when we give a feast, we should invite the poor, the maimed, the lame, the blind – people who can neither pay us back nor do anything for us to deserve it. He was calling us to be merciful and expect our reward at the resurrection of the just.

The resurrection of the just is the resurrection that will bring us to the judgement seat of Christ, where we will be rewarded for the things done in the body, not in the spirit; the latter having been accomplished by the Lord Jesus Christ alone. These are the things we have "in Christ". Afterwards, what we have in Christ must be used now on earth to glorify God the Father. On that day, the merciful will have great rewards.

It takes the demonstration of other virtues of God to show mercy. Virtues like long-suffering, self-control, patience, faithfulness, faith and even love. There is no way we could possibly be merciful without showing these virtues. In 2Peter 1vs5-11, the word of God says, if we have the virtues and abound with them, a great entrance will be supplied to us into the everlasting kingdom of our Lord Jesus Christ. But those who lack them are shortsighted - even blind - to the future qualification into the kingdom of Christ

---

91 2Timothy 1:16-18

on the earth called the Millenial Kingdom of God. All the short-sighted can see is this present evil age. They can only look on things that are visible and temporal now, but cannot look on the things not seen which are eternal.

No wonder after receiving the life of Christ through the new birth, the Lord Jesus Christ said, 'Love you enemies, Bless those who curse you, do good to those who hate you and pray for those who spitefully use you and persecute you.' He further encouraged that if we did this, we would be sons of our Father in Heaven. A son is so called because he is born of the father and so has the life of his father as everything reproduces according to itself. So since in the life of Father God is mercy and love, those born of Him should also express mercy and love.

Remember His word in Luke 6vs36 – Therefore be merciful, just as your Father also is merciful.

Chapter Eight

Blessed Are The pure in Heart

"Blessed are the pure in heart, for they shall see God."

When someone is pure in heart, it means that person has his heart focused on the mind of the Lord.[92] His mind is firmly fixed on the Lord Himself. A double minded believer will struggle to serve the Lord. He first needs his heart to be purified;[93] whereas the single minded believer is focused on the will of God. The natural mind is aganist the will of God and is of the world, of flesh and of the prince of the power of the air - satan. It is all these factors which will make the heart impure.

To explain further, the whole universe was programmed to yield to the will of God alone. Things were like that until one of the angels of God in heaven called *Lucifer* rebelled against the will of God by trying to execute his *own* will. Lucifer's heart became consumed with his own interests as the word of God makes clear -

"For you have said in your heart, I will ascend into heaven; I will exalt my throne above the stars of God; I will also sit on the mount of the congregation on the farthest side of the north, I will ascend above the heights of the cloud, I will be like the Most High.[94]

---

92 Psalm 112:9
93 James 4:8
94 Isaiah 14:13-14

The highlighted statement in the above scripture - *"For you have said in your heart"* - shows that Lucifer's heart was impure as he changed from being God-focused to self-focused. God is the originator of all things in heaven, earth, sea and all the universe. He created them all in response to His own heart's desire and will. Without the intention and desire of God, nothing could exist. We know that God *"created all things and by His will they exist and were created."*[95] Everything was rightfully responding and existing for the purpose and will of God until Lucifer said in his heart words which prioritised his own will and not the will of God. This is called *iniquity*. This kind of heart is an impure heart. The result was that he was driven out of heaven and lost the ability to see God.

In the Garden of Eden, Adam's heart was very pure because he knew nothing but the will of God; and such to the point that even when he and his wife were naked, they were not ashamed. This was because from the beginning, God did not give him the ability to know good and evil and so commanded him to stay away from the *tree of the knowlege of good and evil* – a tree that contained the ability for self knowledge. We could call it the Tree of Death.

Man, as it were, had no knowledge of good and evil, so the ability to be ashamed of nakedness was none existent. The knowledge in man at that time was *solely* God and His will. This made Adam's heart very pure until he partook of the fruit from the tree of the *knowledge* of good and evil. This is the self-gained knowledge that gave Adam the ability to acquire a thinking pattern totally without recourse to God.

When the knowledge of self consciousness was activated, he knew he was naked and became ashamed. His heart became impure and the consequence he suffered was the same as Lucifer's – he was driven out of God's presence, and forfeited the blessing of seeing God.

Those who are born again today were naturally born with an impure heart, contaminated with the will of the flesh and the individual will. We were naturally born with a self-willed heart,

---

95 Revelation 4:11

programmed with the ways of this world and influenced by Satan and his demons (principalities and powers) exerting power over various tribes, tongues, peoples and nations. After we are born again by the Spirit of God, we become double minded. This is because we still have our worldly mind in addition to our *new mind* —the mind of Christ.[96]

The Spirit of God in us wants to move us from double mindedness to single mindedness – a mind focused on God's will alone like the Lord Jesus Christ. For He said *"Most assuredly, I say to you, the Son can do nothing of Himself, but what He sees the Father do, for whatever He does, the Son also does in like manner."*[97] The Spirit of God has already given us the mind of Christ but it needs development to the point where it will have a much stronger influence on you than the mind of the flesh which is your natural mind of self and futility. As we yield ourselves to the Spirit of God, we will be more and more pure in heart because He will lead us into all truth which is the will of God in His Word. He will take of Christ Jesus and declare Him to us; the effect being the blessing of *seeing* God. In other words, the Father will continue to show us the things that He does and even greater things so that people around us can marvel.[98]

The more we see God in this way, the more we will be transformed into the image of Christ, the Son of the living God. The ultimate result is that we will exercise dominion over this earth and rule and reign with Christ in His coming kingdom. Indeed, what a blessing to be pure in heart - a heart not contaminated with the world![99]

A common sign of an impure heart in the believer is that he does not have confidence before God because of the consciousness of his infirmities and sins. He is so conscious of himself that he finds it very difficult to believe that *in* Christ Jesus, he is justified. As Adam hid himself away from God when God asked, *"Adam where are you?"* and in response, he blamed his wife for

---
96 1 Corinthians 1:30, 2 Timothy 1:7
97 John 5:19
98 John 5:20
99 James 4:4; 1 John 2:15-17

his fall, so do these believers condemn themselves before God and cannot believe that God would answer their prayers. They rather find it convenient to blame other people for their mistakes and cannot forgive those who offend them. They are always looking for ways to please God by what they do; they are strangers to the grace of God in Christ Jesus.

Having A Pure Heart

WORD OF GOD

The Holy Spirit will help us remember the scriptures[100] we diligently study in order to cleanse our hearts and keep us from sinning.[101] As we obey the words of the Lord that the Holy Spirit brings to mind, our hearts are cleansed and made pure. But the responsibility is ours to study the scriptures (the word of God in the Bible) and accompany this with prayer. As we pray, not just making requests known to God but praying in the Spirit (as He gives the utterance) and with our understanding, while also assembling together with the saints in our local churches, the Holy Spirit will perform His will in our lives. The book of James encourages us to *"receive the implanted word with meekness."*[102] Many are hearing the word of God without any benefits because they are not receiving it with meekness. They receive it to increase in knowledge to boast about how much they know. Some receive the word of God with a sealed mindset, and if what they hear is not in line with what they have known before, they will reject it. Such people are not receiving the word with meekness but rather with the arrogance and pride which derives from the nature of satan.

In Zephaniah 3:9-12 lies a prophecy regarding our days; when the Spirit has been poured out on us and we have received a pure language enabling us to call upon the Lord in tongues and in praying the word of God in our understanding. We are those

---
100 John 14:26
101 Psalm 119: 9-11
102 James 1:21

who are called the circumcision in Christ who worship God in the Spirit and in Truth; people that the Father has been seeking to worship Him. All this is possible because we are born of God and are in Christ.

But here is the warning in verse 11 and 12, - *"For then I will take away from your midst those who rejoice in your pride and you shall no longer be haughty on My holy mountain. I will leave in your midst a meek and humble people, and they shall trust in the name of the Lord."*

These verses show that it is possible to be on the Holy Mountain of God which is His Presence and still be haughty and proud. Peter also spoke to believers on this wise saying, *"God resists the proud but gives grace to the humble."*[103] This is why the word of God must be received with meekness before you can bear its fruit.

SAVE YOUR SOULS

What is a soul? Our souls are where our mind and emotions are located. The mind of a soul is programmed with all the impurities of self, flesh and the world. But the implanted word of God will save a believer's soul from all the impurities in his mind through the washing of the water of the word.[104] In other words, it washes like water all the impurities of the mind/heart and makes one a man of a pure heart, whose mind is always on the Lord.

This is when our prayers become so effective because all our requests or petitions will be in agreement with the will of God and we will become true intercessors. We no longer pray and ask because it looks good and sounds good, but we pray because it is His will. When we pray in tongues (heavenly language) with a pure heart, we will have the faith that our prayers are effective because of the revelation this utterance grants us by the Holy Spirit. Again He helps us pray according to the undiluted will of God which can never be fully grasped in our limited understand-

---
103 James 4:6
104 Ephesians 5:26

ing. We will then live out the Lord's prayer, which says *"Our Father who art in heaven, hallowed be your name. Your kingdom come, Your will be done on earth as it is in heaven."*[105] We will begin to experience answered prayers as God has promised - *"If you abide in Me, and My words abide in you, you will ask what you desire and it shall be done for you."*[106] At this stage, God can trust your desires because they are all in agreement with His will. You have become pure in heart. The pure in heart see God with their spiritual eyes and have an effective prayer life. This is truly a great blessing! May the Lord give us the ability to appreciate these blessings, though they are not physical or material things that appeal to the natural man.

The believer who is pure in heart or progressing well in acquiring purity of heart may still make mistakes or miss the mark. However, whenever he is prompted, by the Holy Spirit through the scriptures or through fellow believers, of the right way, he is very quick to make the necessary adjustments in a spirit of true repentance. He will not give excuses for his errors. His heart is so fixed on the Lord that he does not care about any shame he will suffer when he admits his errors. He is so unconcerned about his reputation that he is quick to apologise and repent before God.

---

105 Matthew 6:9-10
106 John 15:7, 1 John 5:14-15

Chapter Nine

Blessed Are The Peacemakers

"Blessed are the peacemakers, for they shall be called Sons of God"

Sons of God do not become fully-fledged sons overnight, but make the progression from babies, to children and then grow up to become mature sons.[107] The difference is that children are not responsible but *mature* sons are. You will not entrust your property to your babies or to your children because they may not be responsible as yet. If you do, you will have a lot of things to put right by the time you get home!. They would have turned the entire house upside down. Babies and children care only about their own needs, though they are innocent. But when they grow up to a full understanding of what it means to be a sons, they become responsible and so you can confidently commit your whole property into their hands without any fear or doubt.

In the kingdom of God, it takes a son to be a peacemaker according to the word of God. This is why Paul in 1Corinthians Chapter 3 called the saints in the church *carnal* and *babes* because of the division and contentions among them. The peacemakers in the Kingdom of God are the real builders of the Church - the house of God. They are the ones in the body of Christ who are really the Ministers of Reconciliation.[108] They make peace between all the members of the body of Christ because of their sense of respon-

---
107 Isaiah 9:6
108 2 Corinthians 5:14-19

sibility to build the Church together with the Lord Jesus Christ. They hate to see brothers and sisters fight among themselves. They cannot stand such things as bickering, gossip, envy and jealousy or anything else that promotes disunity in the Church. They have come to the revelation that the Church is *a Person*- Christ the One New Man. His body comprises all true believers in Christ and Jesus Christ Himself is the Head. They know the reality of this and treat all believers with the honour they deserve. So if they observe fights or discord in the body, they see it as an attack against the Lord. Rather than seeing people, they see the Lord who lives in them. They have a pure heart and see the Lord in the Church and in the people of God, unlike those who are still self-centred and impure in heart who do not see the Lord.

Believers who are still at the elementary stage of their maturity, still perceive the church as the world does. They only see individuals who by themselves are supposed to be good. So when the people exhibit bad character, they are offended and seek to distance themselves from the Church and create more division. They have not yet appreciated that *"from Christ Himself, the whole body is joined and knit together by what every joint supplies, according to the effective working by which every part does its share to cause growth of the body for the edifying of itself in love."*[109]

To these childlike believers, the Church is a *place* where they come to meet God who will solve their problems and help them to carry out their own will and plans. They judge their spirituality by how much they have and brag through the testimonies they give in the name of the Lord. They are not concerned about the unity of the body of Christ which will enable the Lord to fully express Himself and His glory on the earth. Soul winning is a strange word to them. In short, they are irresponsible.

Those who promoted envy and strife in the early Church were referred to as babes in Christ and carnal.[110] They are known to preach Christ, but are still babes because they do it with envy and strife. We have a lot of Ministers like that today in the Body

---
109 Ephesians 4:16
110 Philippians 1:15, 1Corinthians 3:1-3

of Christ. To them what matters is not to teach or preach the Person of Christ, but to be '*great*' in this world. They conveniently set aside the full intergrity of God's word.[111] It is clear that there are two kinds of teachers - those who break the commandments and *teach* men so, and those who do the commandments and teach men same.

The law of the kingdom of heaven is in faith and love in Christ Jesus yet there are preachers and teachers who teach and encourage racial and ethnic differences in the Body of Christ, while the Lord says our citizenship is in heaven and that we are not of this world. They forget that we have become a Composite - One New Man in whom is *"no Jew nor Greek, circumcised nor uncircumcised, slave nor free, male nor female but we are all one in Christ and Christ is all and in all."*[112] They even celebrate their ethnic cultures and traditions in the church which result in more distinctions in the Body of Christ.

Just as carnality is evidence that a believer is a spiritual 'babe', spirituality is a sign that a believer is a mature son. A spiritual person's life is marked by selflessness, self-denial life and humility. He always brings peace where there is division because he understands that the house of God stands by the oneness and unity of the people of God. Even more than being saints united in Christ, the church is a Person - the Man Christ Jesus. Remember that you can only have a person in a human body, the same goes with the Body of Christ – You can only have one person in the Body of Christ, namely, Christ Jesus. We are therfore *His* body and no longer ourselves.

Saints of God, we have many unstable people in church today because they have been disappointed by the state of some believers in the church. But they forget that nobody comes into the kingdom perfected in the 'flesh'. Everybody in the Body of Christ today has areas of weaknesses in their flesh to be dealt with by God. It is therefore quite unfair for one believer, on account of strength in some area, to expect all others to be as strong. Do not forget we all have our points of weakness and need God's mercy and grace.

---
111 Matthew 5:19
112 Colossians 3:11

Remember **Galatians 6:1-2** which says **"Brethen if a man is overtaken in any trespass, you who are spiritual restore such a one in a spirit of gentleness, considering yourself lest you also be tempted. Bear on another's burdens and so fulfil the law of Christ"**

Also note that we do not relate to others on the basis of their physical person or status. Our oneness is not in the flesh but in the Spirit, which is in the name of our Lord Jesus Christ.[113] Our flesh is who we *were* before we became born-again in Christ. Our spirit is who we now *are* in Christ after being baptised into Christ Jesus. Jesus prayed that the Father should keep us through His *Name* (not our's nor any other) so that we can be one as He is one.[114] So our oneness and unity is only in the Name God has given to us under heaven which is the name Jesus Christ,[115] and a new name signifies a new identity.

If we still identify ourselves by what we were before coming to Christ, we will still be manifesting some differences among us depending on the differences in those identities. The Father will never deny Jesus Christ an answer to prayer because Jesus Christ never sinned. So His prayer has been answered. But the problem is that we are not walking by faith in *His* identity. We are Christians but still holding unto our old identities which we received through our nationalities, race, gender, religion, social class and family lineage.

Remember that being born again is to be born of God.[116] This is why we now have *Zoe* life in us - eternal life, which is God's kind of life. The peacemakers in the kingdom of God are peacemakers because they have come to the reality of this knowledge and are able to see others the way God sees them. It develops the character of longsuffering in them which is one of the qualities of love.[117] The Lord commanded us to walk worthy of our calling with all longsuffering, the purpose being to preserve the

---

113 2 Corinthians 5:16
114 John 17:11
115 Acts 4:12
116 John 1:12-13
117 1 Corinthians 13:4

"*unity of the Spirit in the bond of peace.*"[118] This is the primary focus of sons of God who are peacemakers.

We cannot escape the fact that there will be differences between us in our flesh as a result of the *sin nature* depending in our upbringing and environment. But *"He that is joined to the Lord is one spirit with Him"*[119] which means we need to ignore, and not be controlled by, our fleshly differences but rather know ourselves by the Spirit according to Christ Jesus. This will involve longsuffering and bearing with one another until we receive our new bodies in the future kingdom of Christ. Those who have taken time to discipline themselves with these truths are mature sons of God. The peacemakers make peace because in doing so, they are fellow workers with the Lord Jesus Christ.[120]

For we find that,

The love of Christ compels us because we judge thus: that if one died for all then all died and He died for all, that those who live should live no longer for themselves, but for Him who died for them and rose again. Therefore from now on, we regard no one according to the flesh. Even though we have known Christ according to the flesh, yet now we know Him thus no longer.

How should we now *know* ourselves?

Therefore if anyone is in Christ, he is a new creation, old things have passed away; behold all things have become new.

The '*old things*' which have passed away includes the old man, the old identity which has been crucified with Christ and done away with. The '*all things*' which are now new are all of God because we *in Christ* are born of God.

---

118 Ephesians 4:1-3
119 1 Corinthians 6:17
120 Ephesians 2:11-16

Chapter Ten

Blessed Are Those Who Are Persecuted For Righteousness' Sake

"Blessed are those who are persecuted for righteousness sake, for theirs is the kingdom of heaven."[121]

If you determine to live righteously in this present evil world you will suffer persecution. The present world operates by the principles and values upheld by the *"prince of the power of the air who is Satan."*[122] We are told that the world is characterised by *"the lust of the flesh, the lust of the eye and the pride of life."*[123] They all emanate from lust and self-exaltation; the root of which is iniquity. Iniquity began with Satan.[124] But when we believers choose to live righteously, we are operating by a different principle called *love*. It is demonstrated by a life of selflessness and self-denial which enables us to *"do all things without selfish ambition or conceit but esteem others better than ourselves."*[125] This life of love is *from* God. Believers are commanded to *"Love one another, for God is love; and everyone who loves is born of God and knows God. He who does not love does not know God, for God is love."*[126]

Persecution involves hostility, ill-treatment, harassment, discrimination and torment from others. These are actions demonstrated

---
121 Matthew 5:10
122 Ephesians 2:2
123 1 John 2:16
124 Isaiah 14:12-14, Ezekiel 28:11-19
125 Philippians 2:3
126 1 John 4:7-8

by people against individuals who exhibit qualities that are not acceptable to them. For people to react that way against a believer, the believer must have behaved, done or said something contrary to what is acceptable to them. Believers who desire to live righteously will suffer persecution because they will be living out the principles of the kingdom of heaven or the kingdom of God which are in direct opposition to the principles of this world.

This world is under the influence of the wicked one satan[127] and all human cultures and traditions are influenced and even programmed by the principalities and powers (satan's army of angels) in the heavenly places. The world operates on the basis of self-exaltation and pride as opposed to the principles of Christ which are based on self-denial through the application of the Cross of Christ in the believer's life. This is the reason for the persecution of a believer who desires to live godly and righteously in Christ Jesus. The persecution may even be within the Church where the principle of self-denial has not been accepted as a way of life for believers, or it may be from your family and the society.

As believers we should arm ourselves with the *mind* of Christ. This means a willingness to suffer in the flesh; the result of which we are *able* to cease from sin.[128] Suffering in the flesh means that we no longer live by the former *identity* we had in the world but now live by the new identity in Christ as a *new man.* Paul told us in the book of Philippians that he suffered in the flesh the *loss* of *all things* accomplished in the flesh so that he might *gain* Christ.

Have a closer look at all the things that Paul counted as loss in Philippians 3 - things he termed *FLESH* - and apply them to your own background. The outcome will be that all your old identity in Adam - all achievement - will all be gone. This will open you up to *put on* Christ and resist the actions and desires of the old identity in Adam. Before we came into Christ, we lived for ourselves and craved to satisfy the desires of our flesh and mind.[129] In those times we were dead to the will of God.

---

127 1 John 5:19.
128 1 Peter 4:1-4
129 Ephesians 2:1-2

We used to live in the flesh the same kind of life that changed Lucifer's identity from an angel to the devil. He was cast down to the earth, never to be part of the kingdom of God. It was the life that puts the self *("I")* before God. These are the words satan said in his heart that caused his fall:

"*I will* ascend to heaven;

I will exalt my throne above the stars of God;

I will also sit on the mount of the congregation on the furtherest side of the north;

I will ascend above the heights of the clouds;

I will be like the Most High."[130]

Even though satan did not create himself, he suddenly decided to disregard God's purpose for his existence and determine his own destiny. He embodied pride and rebellion, self-will and lust, all stemming from iniquity. This same kind of mind can be seen in people today. Since the fall of Adam in the garden of Eden, satan has injected this self-will into man, and it has not only produced separation between God and man but also divisions, wars, fights and various distinctions amongst mankind. Nations have been warring against themselves; people against people.

It is no wonder that satan is called *"The Ruler of Darkness of this World"* since the system of this world is programmed by him.[131] The word of God tells us that Jesus Christ did the exact opposite of what satan and the world are doing. Jesus Christ *"made Himself of no reputation, taking the form of a bondservant, and coming in the likeness of men. And being found in appearance as a man, He humbled Himself and became obedient to the point of death, even the death of the cross."*[132] Jesus Christ already being in the form of God (because He *is* God), willingly descended to the earth as a Man in order to do the will of His Father God. When

---
130 Isaiah 14:13-14
131 Ephesians 6:12
132 Philippians 2:5-8

He was on earth, He did not deserve to die because He never sinned. When His Father revealed to Him His love for mankind and His decision to execute the due judgement of man on Jesus (so that mankind will be saved from eternal damnation,) He did not claim His *right* not to die. This is what the natural man would have done. Instead, He said *"Not as I will but Father your will be done."*

If this is His principle of living, how can we as Christians be in Christ as a new man and expect to live by the same principles of this world? Once you are in Christ, there is no other life in you than the life of self-denial - a life not focused on *your rights* but on the *will* of God. You can only walk in this self-denial if you come to a revelation of Christ and what He has accomplished *for* you and *in* you. The scripture says Christ left us an example to follow. He suffered, not because of any sin or deceit in His life, for which reason he had the right to continue living without death. However he did not exercise this right but rather suffered death because of us. He became *sin* for us to be qualified to receive God's righteousness; He was cursed for us to be blessed. All this was made possible because He lived for His Father's will and not His rights.[133]

Since this is the example He left us, we also should lay down our lives for others, especially, for our brothers and sisters in Christ. We can do this because we have received the same kind of life He has - ZOE, which is eternal life. With this life, which is God's kind of life, we can do what He did.[134] Living in this evil world with the life of Christ (as explained above) will expose you to persecution because you will be in opposition to the powers of the adversary satan.

It is indisputable that all that Jesus has done and all that He commands His disciples and us to do is all for the good and advantage of man. It's all about love and looking out for the good of others. Yet people are against Him and do not want Him in their lives. Even Christians who have the Holy Spirit in them to help them, still struggle to live out this life and even struggle

---
133 1 Peter 2:20-23
134 John 14:12

accepting some of Christ's principles. Yet none of His principles harm us, they are all for our betterment. Clearly, there are powers beyond this physical realm that are in control of man's way of thinking. The same exist to discourage God's principles meant to give life. These are the powers that inspire the natural and carnal man to persecute you when you step out to live a life of self-denial life and obey the words of our Lord Jesus Christ.

Pilate, before whom Jesus was brought for judgement, was not a Jew; but he was a king in Rome, as such, a Gentile king. The Gentiles at that time were the non-believers. By inference therefore, they were *sons of disobedience* in whom the 'prince of the power of the air' was constantly at work. Pilate thus is a *type - a* picture of satan himself ruling the people through worldly authority. So when Jesus stood before Pilate, He was actually standing before the powers of darkness and satan in the invisible realm. So Pilate was not just speaking of his own accord but was under the influence of powers unknown to him. This is why when he wanted to release the Lord Jesus and let him go, he could not. He was forced to authorise the crucifixion of the Lord Jesus Christ. Who was behind the whole event? For in the events preceding the crucifixion Pilate said to the Chief Priests and the crowd *"I find no fault in this Man."*[135]

Speaking through Pilate, satan admitted that there was no fault in Jesus Christ *as a Man*. Earlier on he had tried in the wilderness during Jesus' 40 days of fasting to persuade him to take a decision outside His Father's will and cause Him to sin. He continued to tempt Jesus all through His lifetime on earth with no success. Jesus overcame him so much that even before He was arrested, He said *"the ruler of this world is coming and he has nothing in Me."*[136] Jesus was referring to self-will and self-exaltation, both of which were absent from his heart. He only did the things He *saw* His Father do.[137]

You would logically think that because Jesus was free from satan's influences, He would also be free from satan's assault and

---
135 Luke 23:4
136 16 John 14:30
137 John 5:19

persecution? But it was this aspect of His character which brought Him face to face with the persecution of satan and all his assaults through people. Because He was spotless, satan saw Him as a threat which needed to be eliminated. When you are born-again, you receive the same Spirit of Christ, his divine nature, in which satan finds no fault. This becomes a serious threat to him! Therefore, he will orchestrate persecution against you through people, tough circumstances and challenges in this life. The Lord sought to prepare us for this with these words: " *In the world you will have tribulation; but be of good cheer, I have overcome the world."*[138]

You will never undergo the same suffering of the Lord, no-one can. He has done it once and for all; but the principle of self-denial is still the governing factor of the Christian life. The Lord Himself said *"If anyone desires to come after Me, let him deny himself, and take up his cross and follow Me."*[139] As the time approached for Jesus to be crucified, *"Jesus said to the chief priests, captains of the temple, and the elders who had come to Him, 'Have you come out, as against a robber, with swords and clubs? When I was with you daily in the temple, you did not try to seize Me. But this is your hour, and the power of darkness.' "*[140]

The power of darkness was behind everything and still is behind all the persecution and tribulations of the saints in Christ who desire to go beyond the objective righteousness in Christ and allow Christ to live in and through them to manifest His righteousness by faith. This will involve submissiveness to the Holy Spirit and a mind-set of self-denial.

The Example Of Anna The Prophetess

Anna[141] represents the true intercessors who are the overcoming saints. She had a husband for seven years and then became a widow. Similarly, the overcoming saints who desire to manifest

---

138 John 16:33
139 Matthew 16:24
140 Luke 22:47-53
141 Luke 2:36-38

the righteousness of Christ through a life of self-denial, were once married to this world and its principles of living. The principles and traditions of this world were their 'husband' who ruled over them[142] and controlled their will, but in the seventh year which represents the fullness of the times, the death of Christ separated them from their worldliness and they were taken out of this world and placed into another environment, nation and kingdom called Christ. They were baptised into Christ and became 'a new man', who was created according to God in true righteousness and holiness. In this new environment, they are renewed in knowledge according to the image of Him who created them by means of the resurrection of Jesus Christ from the dead.[143]

The new environment for Anna was the temple of God and that temple today is Christ *Himself*.[144] What was Anna doing in this new environment? She was serving God with prayer and fasting. She was praying for the fulfillment of God's will, namely, Jesus Christ. This is an example of self-denial. Prayer alone can still be motivated by selfishness when it is all focused on people's desires and what they want from God. James described it as *"asking amiss that you may spend it on your pleasures."*[145]

Fasting, the *denial* of physical food, also typifies the denial of our will and desires in order to express the will and desires of the Holy Spirit. This occurs to ensure His *"will is done on earth as it is in heaven"*, and that *His* eternal purpose in Christ might be accomplished on this earth - that Christ be all and in all.[146] These overcoming saints dedicate themselves to selfless prayers in the Spirit and are the true house of God, the *"house of prayer for all nations."*

Anna was persistent for 84 years and her prayers were answered when Jesus Christ was born. However, he suffered persecution immediately following his birth. King Herod commanded all chil-

---

142 Genesis 3:16b
143 1 Peter 1:3
144 Colossians 1:19, Colossians 2:9
145 James 4:3
146 Ephesians 4:10, Ephesians 1:10

dren from two years old below to be killed in order to destroy Jesus Christ. Can you see that wherever Christ is revealed in this world persecution follows? Those who endure without being offended will receive a great reward in the kingdom of heaven. As the overcoming saints pray in the Spirit and Christ is revealed through their prayers, they understand and rejoice at the persecution because they see beyond this present evil world.

Is this not how Paul lived his life as a bondservant of Jesus Christ and became an overcomer? He described himself as having to *"labour in birth again until Christ is formed in you."*[147] To gain Christ was so much his focus that he was willing to suffer the loss all things that he had gained in the flesh, which formerly, had been his source of confidence.[148] But he had a revelation that they were all rubbish and was therefore willing to release them all for one purpose - to *gain* Christ. This is the mindset of the true intercessors and overcomers.

The Sign Of The Woman Of Revelation 12

"A great and wondrous sign appeared in heaven: a woman clothed with the sun, with the moon under her feet and a crown of twelve stars on her head. She was pregnant and cried out in pain as she was about to give birth." v1-2

"When the dragon saw that he had been hurled to the earth, he pursued the woman who had given birth to the male child. The woman was given the two wings of a great eagle, so that she might fly to the place prepared for her in the desert, where she would be taken care of for a time, times and half a time, out of the serpent's reach." v13-14

The following are the types and symbols described in this passage[149] and their interpretations and relevance to Christians today:

---

147 Galatians 4:19
148 Philippians 3:8
149 Revelation 12: 1-6, 13-14

The woman represents the overcoming saints.

The moon symbolises the *'ruler of the darkness of this world'*- satan and his fallen angels. The reason is that the moon, from the account of Genesis Chapter 1, rules the night, and night represents the dark hour of the day.

The woman has on her head a garland of twelve Stars - the number twelve stands for nation - the Holy Nation.[150]

The garland which is a crown stands for the authority of kingship.

Her labour pains symbolise a priestly ministry of intercession in order to give birth to the Christ.

The sun represents the Sun of Righteousness[151] who is Christ Jesus our Lord. She was *clothed with the Sun* - These are the saints who have learnt by faith to put on Christ after being *baptised into* Him. Their identity is now in Christ as a new man and they can be all things to all men on earth for soul winning. In the Church, they are neither black nor white; neither Jew nor Greek; neither slave nor free; neither 'African church' nor 'White church' etc., but Christ is their *clothing* – their identity.

The account of creation informs us that the moon rules the night which is the dark hour of the day.[152] These evil powers including satan are under the feet of the overcomers who have clothed themselves with Christ and are walking on earth as strangers and pilgrims because they have accepted the life of self-denial in Christ. Believers can only give birth to the image of Christ as a result of the ministry of intercession. The saints who are the first fruit of the Spirit are groaning within themselves, eagerly anticipating their adoption - the redemption of their body.[153]

"The Dragon stood before her" – That dragon is satan and he fights against these overcomers who represent a royal priest-

---
150 1 Peter 2:9
151 Malachi 4:2
152 Genesis 1:16
153 Romans 8:29

hood and a holy nation. This is so because they are bringing forth fruit. Satan does not want Christ to take His rightful place on this earth. This is confirmed in the passage which poses the question:

"Why do the nations rage and the people plot a vain thing? The kings of the earth set themselves and their rulers take counsel together against the Lord and against His Anointed (His Christ), saying Let us break their bonds in pieces and cast away their cords from us."[154]

Satan's chief aim is to abort the vision of Christ in believers. This he does by planting the seed of individualism and self-centredness within their hearts in order to break the the unity of the Spirit in the bond of peace. He fails when overcomers deny themselves and instead choose the eternal Zoe kind of life they have in Christ. All selfish ambition and lust for the things of this world are herein crucified with Christ.

'The woman is clothed with the sun' Such is the identity of the overcomers because they have given up their own identities to gain Christ, and have confessed that they are strangers and pilgrims on this earth.[155] They know that because they are baptised into Christ, they have put on Christ[156] and so there is no more place for the flesh.[157] The result was that the woman gave birth to that which was of Christ and it was immediately caught up to God in heaven because it was incorruptible - a treasure laid up for them in heaven. What immediately followed was persecution, but God prepared a place for her.

Beware Of The Way Of Cain

Cain and Abel both brought their sacrifices to God.[158] Apparently they were both conscious of the existence of God and the need

---

154 Psalm 2:1-2
155 Hebrews 11:13-16
156 Galatians 3:27
157 Romans 6:3-11
158 Genesis 4:1-9

to worship and honour Him, and they were also both aware of the right time to worship God with their sacrifice. Their father Adam may have taught them what to sacrifice to God. Hebrews reveals that *"By faith Abel offered a more excellent sacrifice than Cain."*[159] So Abel did it *by faith*. Therefore to have done this by faith presupposes that the word of God must have come to them first; for faith can only come by hearing the word of God.[160] The word of God therefore *came to* them both. God is no respecter of persons and sows the seed of His word not only in the good ground but also by the wayside, rocky ground and among thorns, knowing only the good ground will bear fruit.[161] So Cain and Abel both received the word of faith about what to sacrifice to God, but the word was only of benefit to Abel because he allowed the word to produce faith in him.

Abel represents the company of God's people who are saved by their faith in the offered blood of Jesus Christ and are saved by grace and continue to walk with God. Abel brought to God the first born of his flock and of their fat. This represents God's own sacrifice for sin which people have to accept by denying themselves and applying the blood of the sacrifice. God sees those who accept Jesus' sacrifice for sin on the cross as righteous. But Cain represents the company of people who are religious and would only approach God with their own righteousness and on their own terms.

These may even perform good deeds and give out their goods but not in love.[162] Cain brought to God an offering of the fruit of the ground. This represents the sweat of his face out of the cursed ground, cursed because of his knowledge of good and evil[163]. This is why God said his works were evil.[164] With this sacrifice, Cain was not denying himself and submitting to the way of the cross of Christ. He was doing something out of his own wisdom that would enable him have something to boast about before God. This God did not accept and will not accept. Although he heard

---
159 Hebrews 11:4
160 Romans 10:17
161 Matthew 13:1-9
162 1 Corinthians 13:3
163 Genesis 3:17-19
164 1 John 3:12

the same word as Abel his brother, he would not submit to the word of God and still insisted on approaching God on his terms. This is why God disrespected his sacrifice. We can see this mindset in many religious groups in the world today. They do many good deeds but still reject the Son of God - God's own precious sacrifice for them. God called such works evil. Jesus made it very clear in His word - "*I am the Way, the Truth, and the Life; no one comes to the Father but by Me.*"[165] The Outcome was that Cain murdered Abel his brother, yet another example of persecution from those who are religious but not truly spiritual like Cain.

---

165 John 14:6, 1 John 5:12

CHAPTER ELEVEN

THE CROWN RECEIVERS

You therefore must endure hardship as a good soldier of Jesus Christ. No one engaged in warfare entangles himself with the affairs of this life, that he may please him who enlisted him as a soldier. And also if anyone competes in athletics, he is not crowned unless he competes according to the rules.[166]

From the scripture stated above, these are the rules guiding any athlete for the competitors to follow in order to be crowned with rewards. If the rules are broken, even if an athlete comes top on the list, he will be disqualified because he has not run according to the rules. The Apostle Paul who by the Holy Spirit wrote these words down in the bible actually competed according to the rules because at the end of his life on earth, he was certain that he would be crowned by the Lord Himself as he stated:

For I am already being poured out as a drink offering, and the time of my departure is at hand. I have fought the good fight, I have finished the race, I have kept the faith. Finally, there is laid up for me the crown of righteousness, which the Lord, the righteous Judge, will give to me on that Day, and not to me only but also to all who have loved His appearing.[167]

---
166 2 Timothy 2:3-5
160 2 Timothy 4:6-8

The crown that Paul received was the Crown of righteousness. This, I believe, is the imperishable crown that successful and overcoming saints will receive on that Day. 1Corinthians 9:25 tells us that we are competing for an imperishable crown. This signifies a reward that will never perish but is eternal; which is far better than any reward that can be received in this world.

How To Recieve

"And everyone who competes for the prize is temperate in all things." [168]

Also in 1Cornithians 9:27 the word of God says:

"But I discipline my body and bring it into subjection, lest, when I have preached to others, I myself should become disqualified."

To be temperate (discipline of the body) and bringing it (body) into subjection all signify self control or endurance. We must be able to endure to qualify for this imperishable crown of righteousness. This is why we are encouraged to endure hardship and also not to engage in the affairs of this life in order to please the Lord Jesus and be His good soldiers.[169] Paul, who said he had finished his race and had a crown of righteousness laid up for him by the Lord, really lived a life of hardship and endurance to obtain this reward. The Holy Spirit revealed to him that chains and tribulations awaited him in Jerusalem, but Paul was not discouraged by that prophesy, instead, he said that none of those things moved him.[170] He did not count his life so dear as to lose sight of Christ. Why? So he might finish his race and keep the ministry he had received from the Lord.

Can you see that endurance is a great key to fulfilling divine destiny and receiving rewards from the Lord? No wonder Paul said he had to press on so that he might lay hold of that for which Christ

---

168 1Corinthians 9:25
169 2 Timothy 2:3-4
170 Acts 20:23-24

Jesus had intended for him.[171] Of course, Christ Jesus had already secured him as *'complete in Christ'* in the heavenly places[172] but *on earth*, he had to press through the attractions and distractions of the flesh, the deeds of the body, in order to live out what Christ Jesus had accomplished on the cross.

The word **PRESS** involves endurance and self control. *"I press toward the goal for the prize of the upward call of God in Christ Jesus."*[173] The prize is the imperishable crown as we have established above but in order to get it, he had to press; meaning there was a force acting against him, hence it involved pressing through. Consequently, we cannot successfully press without temperance and endurance.

What was Paul pressing through? - the deeds of the body in the flesh, because:

"For the flesh lusts against the Spirit, and the Spirit against the flesh; and these are contrary to one another, so that you do not do the things that you wish." [174]

"For if you live according to the flesh you will die (no reward); but if by the Spirit you put to death the deeds of the body, you will live (reward)." [175]

This is why he disciplined himself and put his body in subjection.[176]

There is even a promise from the Lord to those who keep His command to persevere. It is to keep them from the hour of trial that would come upon the whole world to test those who dwell on the earth.[177] To preserve is a command according to this scripture and every command kept shows obedience which, expectedly, brings blessings and reward.

---

171 Philippians 3:12-14
172 Colossians 2 vs 10
173 Philippians 3:14
174 Galatians 5:17
175 Romans 8:13
176 1 Corinthians 9:27
177 Revelation 3:10

Also we know that an *entrance* will be supplied into the everlasting kingdom of our Lord Jesus Christ for those who not only had faith but also would add to their faith, virtue, knowledge, self control, perseverance, Godliness, brotherly kindness and love.[178] All these qualities are not gifts but characters of Christ that have to be developed as we yield to the workings of the Holy Spirit in our hearts.

Bear in mind that our ultimate destiny is to be conformed to the image of Christ Jesus. It is a destiny assigned to us before the foundation of the world by God who *foreknew* and *predestined* us. No matter what affliction we go through as believers, they are all considered *light* afflictions, which are only temporal and are working out for us a far more exceeding and eternal weight of glory.[179]

Why Endure?

This is because all the commands of Christ as spoken by Him in Matthew 5, 6 and 7, which are the life style or the moral acts of the Kingdom of Christ, can only be lived by those who have the life of the Son of God through the new birth. But after the new birth, this life of God's Son is only in our spirit while the soul and body are still left *in the condition* they were before the new birth.

Therefore there is a continual battle in the believer to neglect the deeds of the former life in the body and be renewed in his mind, which is in the soul, in order to obey and yield to his spirit which is one with the Lord Himself.[180] If you take time to study all the laws of Christ in Matthew 5, 6 and 7, you will see that a man *without* Christ can never practise what Jesus Christ commanded. Likewise, a man in Christ who has not yielded his mind to God's word, which is able to save his soul,[181] will be unable to do them.

---

178 2 Peter 1:5-11
179 2 Corinthians 4:17
180 1 Cornithians 6:17
181 James 1:21

It takes only those who are humble and tremble at the word of the Lord[182] to obey those commandments. So we must not be sluggish but imitate *"those who by faith and patience (endurance) inherit the promise"*[183] We do not draw back to perdition but are among those who believe to the saving of our souls.[184] The Lord Jesus Christ Himself has set us such an example to follow: *"Looking unto Jesus, the author and finisher of our faith, who for the joy that was set before Him endured the cross, despising the same and has sat down at the right hand of the throne of God"* (reward). *For consider Him who endured such hostility from sinners against Himself, lest you become weary and discouraged in your souls. You have not yet resisted to bloodshed, striving against sin.*[185]

Be Encouraged

Those light afflictions are only but for a moment (temporal) and are *"working out for us a far more exceeding and external weight of glory while we do not look at the things which are seen, but at the things which are not seen. For the things which are seen are temporal, but the things which are not seen are eternal."*[186] Verse 18 tells us where to focus our souls/hearts in order to overcome.

These eternal things are the *"hope set before us* that gives joy in the midst of trials. They are the *"things to come"* which is our promised land - Canaan; the millennial reign of Christ on earth with the overcomers. **THIS IS THE DESTINY FULFILLMENT** awaiting us as spoken by the Holy Spirit.[187] Before Elijah was taken up, all the sons of the prophets and Elisha knew that he would be taken up. However, there was *one thing* known only to Elisha and not to the others - such that motivated Elisha to endure and follow his master all the way through Jordan - *to see* Elijah taken up to heaven. This was **The Knowledge Of The Await-**

---
182 Isaiah 6:1-2
183 Hebrew 6:12
184 Hebrews 10:39
185 Hebrews 12:2-4
186 2 Corinthians 4:17
187 Hebrew 2:5-9

ing Reward Of The Mantle From Elijah. The mantle was only for those who would follow him all through from *Gilgal* to *Bethel*; and *Jericho* through *Jordan*. The latter means death – death to the world through the Cross; from where we receive life that is from above in CHRIST.

This reward the sons of the prophets knew not, hence they backed off, thinking that nothing could come out of enduring to the end.

"He that endures to the end shall be saved."[188]

"You shall be hated for my names sake."[189]

We as believers were baptised into His Name (Jesus Christ) to be saved for the remission of sins[190]; but are we willing to *put on* the name **Christ** as our identity here on earth? Are we willing to suffer hatred for His name sake - being rejected by the world? Will we pay the price to gain heavens acceptance? To be counted worthy of the kingdom of God will take faith and patience (endurance) in the midst of persecution and tribulations.

It is no wonder the scriptures say,

"Through many tribulations, we must enter the kingdom of God."[191]

---

188 Matthew 24:3
189 Matthew 24:9, Luke 6:22
190 Acts 2:38
191 Acts 14:22

Conclusion

The Lord Jesus Christ has a great desire for you to reign and rule with Him in His coming kingdom on this earth for a thousand years. This is your true destiny in life. From the beginning, you were created by God to first, be in His image and likeness and then, as those in the image and likeness of God, to exercise dominion on the earth. Even the whole earth and its atmosphere have been programmed by God to yield in submission to those in the image and likeness of God. This why Jesus Christ did great wonders on earth and He exercised dominion over all created things on earth and its atmosphere.

God's next agenda, after the resurrection of the Lord Jesus Christ and His ascension back to the Father, is to bring many sons into the glory of Jesus Christ, to reign and rule with Him and so fulfil His word. We are called *heirs* of God and also *co-heirs* with Christ. But we are only co-heirs if we suffer with Him; thus can we be glorified with Him.

Before we can be qualified for this glory with Christ, we have to be conformed to the image and likeness of God. The present humanity inhabiting the earth is *not* in the image of God but in the image of satan who works in the sons of disobedience.[192]

Before you can be moulded into the image and likeness of God, you must go through a process that will involve being *poor* in spirit, mourning, meekness, hungering and thirsting for righteousness (subjective righteousness), being merciful, pure in heart, becoming a peacemaker and suffering persecution for righteousness sake. It explains why the word of God says, *"We

---
192 Ephesians 2:2; 5:6, Colossians 3:6

must through many tribulations enter the kingdom of God."[193]

The Apostle Peter greeted the Elders in the church by saying - "The Elders who are among you I exhort, I who am a fellow Elder and a witness of the sufferings of Christ, and also a partaker of the glory that will be revealed."[194] He was able to confidently say that he would share in the glory *to be revealed* (Future tense), which is the glory of the Lord Jesus Christ on earth. Similarly, we may take comfort from the promise that "If you are reproached for the name of Christ, blessed are you, for the Spirit of glory and of God rests upon you."[195]

I therefore encourage you fellow strangers and pilgrims on this earth,[196] do not grow weary and discouraged by the afflictions of these days because they are all working for you an exceeding and eternal weight of glory, only as you do not look at the present things you see in this present physical world but look at the things you do not see in this present physical world - things that are invisible now but real in Christ Jesus for you. Because the things you see in this present physical world are all temporary and will perish but the things you do not see in this present physical world that are real in Christ for you are eternal and they will earn you great honour and reward before the Lord.[197]

---

193 Acts 14:22
194 1 Peter 5:1
195 1 Peter 4:14
196 1 Peter 2:11
197 2 Corinthians 4: 16

Appendix A

Praying The Word

For a Christ-like Character

Praise, thanks, honour and blessed be the God and Father of our Lord Jesus Christ who according to His abundant mercy has begotten me again to a living hope through the resurrection of Jesus Christ from the dead to an inheritance incorruptible and undefiled and that does not fade away reserved in heaven for me. For I am kept by the power of God through faith for salvation ready to be revealed in this last time.

I now rejoice in this salvation though now for a little while, if need be, I experience grief by various trials so that the geniuness of my faith, being much more precious than gold that perishes, though it is tested by fire will be found to praise, honour and glory at the revelation of Jesus Christ. For though having not seen I love; though now I do not see Him, yet believing, I rejoice with joy inexpressible and full of glory, receiving the end of my faith which is the salvation of my soul. Therfore I will always prosper in *all* things and be in good health in Jesus name.

Everlasting Heavenly Father, because I can do all things through Christ who strengthens me, I gird up the loins of my mind, being sober and rest my hope fully upon the grace that is to be brought to me at the revelation of Jesus Christ. As an obedient child, I do not conform myself to the former lusts in my ignorance but as **YOU** are Holy, let me also be holy in all my conduct. I have put off my former conduct - *the old man* which grows corrupt according to deceitful lust; I am therefore renewed in the spirit of my mind as I put on the new man which was created according to God in the true righteousness and holiness.

Heavenly Father, I give thanks to You that I am the salt of the earth and the light of the world being of one spirit with **YOU**. Because I can do all things through Christ who strengthens me, my righteousness exceeds the righteousness of the Scribes and Pharisees. Therefore I will not be angry with my brother/sister without cause and will not call him/her *'Raca'* (a fool). Neither shall I describe anyone by such terms but rather my speech will always be with grace, seasoned with salt so that I will answer everyone rightly and impart grace to my hearers.

Christ is my strength; therefore I will not succumb to lust. I will be faithful to my spouse. My desire is to speak the truth at all times; I will not be vengeful but will overcome evil with good; I will love my enemies, bless those who curse me and do good to those who hate me. I will pray for those who spite me and persecute me; all these I will do because *I am born of God* and possess the eternal life of God in me through Christ Jesus my Lord.

As I can do all things through Christ who strengthens me, all my charitable deeds, prayers and fasting - indeed all my worship - is solely to you. I will always lay up my treasures in heaven where my citizenship belongs.

As a stranger and pilgrim whose citizenship is in heaven, I will not be surprised at the fierce trials that come my way but will rejoice that I could partake of Christ's sufferings. When His glory is subsequently revealed, I will also be glad with exceeding joy! I therefore choose to go through the narrow gate - the difficult way that leads to life - for I am more than a conqueror through Him that loved me.

I will serve God and not mammon, (the riches of this world) because God will always supply all my need *according to His riches in glory by Christ Jesus.*

I can do all things through Christ who strengthens me, hence I will first seek the Kingdom of God and His righteousness, for all other things shall be added to me. I will never lack any good thing because the Lord is my Shepherd, the good Shepherd who gave His life for the sheep.

Amen.

For Abundant Life

Father, I thank You for the Blood of Christ that has been shed for the remission of my sins and now I stand before You boldly as *the righteousness of God in Christ Jesus* in the Holiest of All by the Blood of Jesus.

Father, today I draw near to You with a sincere heart and in the full assurance of faith, having my heart sprinkled from an evil conscience by the sprinkling Blood of Christ and my body washed with the pure water of Your word.

Dear Heavenly Father, I confess that I have been *baptised into* Christ Jesus, and so baptised into his death. I have thus been buried with Him *through* baptism unto death; so that as Christ was raised from the dead by the glory of the Father, even so do I *walk* in newness of life. As I am in His death *even so am I now* in His resurrection, being raised up *together* and seated *together* in the Heavenly places with Christ Jesus. Since I have died with Christ Jesus, I am now free from sin.

As I know and believe by faith that Christ was raised from the dead *once for all* and He dies no more, even so am I raised from the dead with Christ. I die no more; death no longer has dominion over me. Instead I now have life - and that more abundantly.

Again since I have the **SON OF GOD** in whom is life, I have life.

Dear Holy Father, grant me, according to the riches of Your glory, to be strengthened with might through Your Spirit in my inner man so that Christ will dwell in my heart through faith. Being rooted and grounded in love, I will be able to comprehend with all the saints, what is the width and length and depth and height; to know the love of Christ which passes knowledge, to be filled with all the fullness of God.

My loving Father, give me the spirit of wisdom and revelation in the knowledge of Christ. May the eyes of my understanding be enlightened to know what is the hope of Your calling; what are the riches of the glory of Your inheritance in me as a saint and what is the exceeding greatness of Your power towards me as a believer. This is according to the working of Your mighty power which You worked in Christ, when You raised Him from the dead and seated Him at Your right hand in the Heavenly places, far above all principality and power and might and dominion and every name that is named, not only in this age but also in that which is to come.

Father direct my heart into the love of God and into the patience of Christ.

Strengthen me with all might according to Your glorious power, so I could have all patience and longsuffering with joy.

Father, my soul will not cling to the dust so revive me according to Your word in Jesus name.

My soul will not melt from heaviness, but strengthen me according to Your word. Revive me O Lord, for Your names sake and for Your righteousness sake bring my soul out of trouble.

Teach me Your ways and I will walk in Your truth and speak the truth in love so that I will grow up in all things into Christ Jesus, the Head of the Church.

Let the sharing of my faith become effective by granting me boldness to always acknowledge the truth and every good thing which is in me in Christ Jesus.

I confess that I am strong. The word of God is living and abidingly working effectively in me and I have overcome the wicked one, satan himself, and all his demons because greater is He that is in me than he that is in the world. Therefore *I have and will always overcome* satan and all his evil spirits, in Jesus Christ name.

I am of God and though the whole world lies under the rule of the wicked one I have overcome the world.

I am a fellow citizen with the saints and a member of the household of God.

In Christ I am circumcised with the circumcision made without hands, by putting off the body of the sins of the flesh by the *circumcision of Christ*, because I have been *buried with Him* in baptism and *raised with Him* through faith in the working of God who raised Him from the dead.

I am redeemed by the Blood of Jesus Christ and I am a king and priest of God. My citizenship is in heaven from where I am eagerly waiting for the Saviour, the Lord Jesus Christ who will transform my lowly body to be conformed to His glorious body according to His ability to subdue all things to Himself. Because I believe in the Lord Jesus Christ as the scripture has said, out of my belly will continually flow rivers of living water.

Thank You Father for giving me the Spirit of power, love, and a sound mind.

Dear Lord, You do not give aid to angels but to the *seed* of Abraham. I am of Christ, therefore I am Abraham's seed and heir according to the promise, therefore I am qualified for all the help available to me at the throne of grace.

Therefore I, by faith, ask for the:

Spirit of Grace and Supplications

Spirit of Love, Joy and Peace

Spirit of Consolation, Prophecy and Revelation

Spirit of Counsel and Sound mindedness

Spirit of Truth, Wisdom and Knowledge

Spirit of Faith and Creative Spirit in Jesus name.

In Jesus Name, I reject *"the law of the spirit of sin and death"* and stagnation; fear, discouragement and torment; discontentment and evil imagination; rebellion and confusion; error, foolishness and ignorance; doubt, sickness and defeat; void and emptiness.

I confess that in Jesus name, today, I will not stumble in word but speak the truth in Love that I may grow up in all things in Him who is Christ, the perfect Man. I will trust you to bridle my whole body. Therefore, the word of Christ will richly dwell in me and in my heart.

I ask all these in Jesus' Name. Amen.

Now, pray (in tongues) as the Spirit enables you.